BYZANTINE PAINTING

BYZANTINE PAINTING

HISTORICAL AND CRITICAL STUDY BY ANDRÉ GRABAR

SKIRA

RIZZOLI
NEW YORK

Color plate on the title page:

The City of Nazareth. 14th century. Detail of a mosaic
in the outer narthex, church of Kahrieh Djami, Constantinople

✳

© 1979 by Editions d'Art Albert Skira S.A., Geneva
First edition © 1953 by Editions d'Art Albert Skira, Geneva

This edition published in the United States of America in 1979 by

RIZZOLI INTERNATIONAL PUBLICATIONS, INC.
712 Fifth Avenue New York 10019

Translated by Stuart Gilbert

PRINTED IN SWITZERLAND

W E of the twentieth century have learnt to appreciate beauty under all its many aspects; not only those complying with the rules of Greek art formulated in the age of Pericles but also those of other, sometimes very different, civilizations. Thus after our books on Etruscan and Roman Painting, we follow up with a volume dealing with Byzantine Painting, for whose full enjoyment modern art has prepared the way and whose beauties of form and style have indeed a strikingly contemporary appeal.

*

We are all the more convinced of the present need for such a book as this because there is no place in the world today where works that illustrate all the various manifestations of Byzantine pictorial art can be seen together. In this volume the reader will find the treasure trove of prolonged travels in Turkey, Greece, Italy and Jugoslavia as well as visits to the great European museums and libraries.

*

In the course of these expeditions which often took them to faraway, all but inaccessible villages and monasteries, our technicians have photographed, by the direct color separation process, a host of works that, for the most part, have never until now been reproduced in color.

*

The making of this book, which owes so much to the wholehearted co-operation of that eminent expert on Byzantine art and culture, Mr André Grabar, has been rendered possible by the good offices of many persons in authority and institutes; notably His Eminence Cardinal Tisserant and Monsignor Albareda, Director of the Vatican Library; M. Jean Porcher, Curator of the Département des Manuscrits and Mlle M.-T. d'Alverny, Librarian of the Bibliothèque Nationale, Paris; the Directors of Fine Arts at Milan, Palermo, Ravenna, Rome and Venice; the Department of Ancient Monuments in Greece, Mr A. Xyngopoulos, Rector of the University of Salonica, and Mr M. Chatzidakis, Curator of the Benaki Museum in Athens; the Federal Institute for the Preservation of Historical Monuments at Belgrade and its former director Mr R. Ljubinkovic; the Byzantine Institute of America and its Field Director in Istanbul, Professor Paul Underwood; Mr Aziz Bey Ogan, Director of the Archaeological Museum in Istanbul; Mr Ramazanoglu, Curator of the Museum of St Sophia in Istanbul; M. André Chamson, Curator of the Petit Palais in Paris. To all alike we tender our most sincere and grateful thanks for their unfailing kindness and generous assistance.

AUSTRIA

PARIS

SWITZERLAND

GENEVA

FRANCE

CASTELSEPRIO

VENICE

TORCELLO

SOF

RAVENNA

FLORENCE

ITALY

Adriatic

Mediterranean Sea

ROME

COSENZA

PALERMO

CEFALU

This map shows the extensive journeys undertaken by our technicians in order to photograph the Byzantine works of art reproduced in this volume. In the course of their visits to churches, monasteries and famous libraries in Italy, Jugoslavia, Turkey and Greece, they covered a distance of over 6000 miles.

HUNGARY

RUMANIA

BELGRADE

ACANICA

ANI

MILESEVO

STUDENICA

JUGOSLAVIA

BULGARIA

Black Sea

SKOPLJE

ALBANIA

NEREZI

OCHRID

SALONICA

ISTANBUL

TURKEY

OSSANO

GREECE

TURKEY

DAPHNI

CHIOS

MISTRA

ATHENS

ST DEMETRIOS, PROTECTOR OF CHILDREN. SEVENTH CENTURY (?). MOSAIC,
CHURCH OF ST DEMETRIOS, SALONICA.

CONTENTS

BYZANTINE PAINTING

BYZANTIUM, Constantinople, Istanbul are the names borne successively by the great city on the Bosporus which was the headquarters of the art dealt with in the present work. While, keeping to the common practice, we call this art Byzantine, we do not overlook the fact that this epithet is very largely a matter of convention and requires some explanation.

Thus it should be understood that when speaking of Byzantine painting we refer to works that chronologically belong to a period during which the city on the Bosporus had ceased to bear the name "Byzantium" and was called "Constantinople." In fact, paradoxically enough, Byzantine painting came into being on the day when Byzantium itself ceased—officially—to exist. However, this seeming anomaly need not detain us; actually the epithet "Byzantine" could not be replaced by "Constantinopolitan," since the former comprises all the art manifestations in the far-flung Empire whose capital was Constantinople, and the latter is confined to the output of the capital itself. It seems hardly necessary to add that the Empire in question was the Christian State which lasted from 330 to 1453, but not the Mohammedan Empire which succeeded it, though the capital (under the name of Istanbul) remained the same.

As applied to painting and to art in general, the epithet "Byzantine" does not always cover the same field, and it seems desirable to clear up this point also before proceeding further. Some have thought fit to limit its application to works produced in Byzantium, i.e. Constantinople, itself and in the area under its direct influence; and to draw a distinction between Byzantine art thus localized and contemporary productions in other art centers of the Empire and neighboring lands. But, given the limitations of our present knowledge and the relatively small number of extant monuments, this method involves insuperable difficulties. How, indeed, can we appraise the characteristics of Byzantine painting in the strict sense of the term during the fourth, fifth and even the sixth centuries, when all we have to go on as regards this early period is a single example of monumental painting (the decorative mosaics of St Sophia) and a single painted book, the *Natural History* of Dioscorides (at the Vienna library)—which, moreover, is merely a copy of an Alexandrian work? It is only from the ninth century onwards that the distinctive features of the painting whose chief center was the capital of the Byzantine Empire can be determined with any certainty, since it is only then that we have enough works of art, Byzantine and others, to enable us to make the necessary differentiations. Obviously this must not be taken to mean that early Byzantine art lacked characteristics of its own, but it is no easy matter to decide what was specifically Byzantine as against the work, more or less akin to it, produced in Rome, Ravenna, Jerusalem, Alexandria and Antioch, not to mention Salonica and Ephesus, cities which, being in closer touch with Constantinople, may well have come under the direct influence of the art of the metropolis at a very early date.

Thus we have always thought it best to give the term "Byzantine" a wider, more elastic application, and this method will be followed in the present work. In the same way as works of art produced in distant parts of the Empire under Roman government are styled "Roman," the epithet "Byzantine" will be applied to paintings made in countries around the Mediterranean basin subsequently to the transfer of the seat of empire to Constantinople, without implying that these paintings necessarily drew inspiration from Byzantium. True (and here, too, we shall adopt the method followed as regards the art of the Roman epoch immediately preceding it), preference will be given to works which for various reasons seem more closely associated with Byzantium, and we shall leave out of account those which evidently continue or revive local art traditions that had existed prior to the foundation of Constantinople, or which no less evidently were creations of an art remote from the capital. I have in mind the mosaics in some Italian churches (for example Sts Cosmas and Damian at Rome and the chapel of Sant'Aquilino in San Lorenzo's at Milan), the mosaic pavements at Antioch and in Palestine, and the frescos in Coptic monasteries. Though these belong to the Byzantine epoch, being contemporary with the political supremacy of Constantinople and produced for the most part in towns and provinces under the rule of Byzantium, they are works which what little we know of Constantinopolitan art during this period justifies us in excluding from the category of Byzantine art.

There are, however, a number of so to speak intermediate works of the fifth, sixth and seventh centuries whose connection with Byzantium, though unproven, seems more probable. Cases in point are most of the mosaics at Ravenna and Parenzo, various frescos in Santa Maria Antiqua and other Roman churches of the very early Middle Ages, and also some illuminations in Greek sixth-century manuscripts whose place of origin is unknown. Usually we assimilate these works to Byzantine art, not because we regard them as necessarily inspired by the art of Constantinople (an influence incapable of proof) but because, in various degrees, the art they stand for must have been akin to that of the Byzantine capital. A priori we have no difficulty in thus regarding the Greek works of Asia Minor, Syria and Egypt, and needless to say the Balkan peninsula—for the obvious reason that Byzantine culture throughout its course was nourished by the traditions and activities of the Greek communities resident in the East-Mediterranean area. But the inhabitants of the Adriatic and Tyrrhenian littorals, the many Levantines who had settled there and even the Latins, were in too frequent contact with the *pars orientalis* of the Empire and its culture for their Christian art not to be reciprocally affected by that of the Mediterranean cities lying further East, from Salonica and Constantinople to Jerusalem and Sinai. Thus there are grounds for including in the category of works we call Byzantine (though their exact kinship with the art of Constantinople itself cannot be determined) the monumental paintings of the fourth, fifth and sixth centuries found in various Mediterranean regions from the Holy Land to Italy inclusively—and even farther West. Faulty though it may be, this method has history to support it. Until the Lombard conquests in Italy and those of the Mohammedans in the East, and even after the seventh century, there was such constant and close intercourse between all the inhabitants of the Mediterranean lands—and notably those which actively promoted the interests of the Church—that the arts prevailing in these regions, and in particular Christian painting, tended constantly to "pool" their programs, forms and technical procedures; or, to say the least, their practices and innovations ran on parallel lines. Needless to say, this did not rule out local idioms; indeed, in the political and even in the religious life of the various countries around the Mediterranean basin, as in their art, we find very different trends operating simultaneously. But beneath these local divergences there was a common basis and a wide one, and thanks to this, though prototypes are not available, we can picture, if not the works themselves, at least the general nature of the painting at Byzantium between the fourth and sixth centuries, in the light of paintings of the period found in other places. Obviously, since no concrete examples of the works created in Byzantium itself are available, we cannot precisely determine in what respects these differed from the other works of the period produced elsewhere. Nevertheless we are justified in holding that the *koinē*, or common language, of Byzantine art and its leading characteristics are revealed outside the capital sufficiently clearly for us to feel assured that in Constantinople too these constituted the basic language of art and can therefore rightly be styled Byzantine.

However, before we attempt to define this language, it may be well to prepare the ground by distinguishing between the two periods mentioned above; for the scope we give the term "Byzantine" is not the same for the earlier period and for that beginning in the ninth century.

BYZANTINE ART: ITS SIGNIFICANCE AND SCOPE

FIRST PERIOD

The scope of Byzantine painting during the early phase may be defined chronologically and geographically as follows. Since in the absence of Constantinople as the constant and primordial center of a specific Christian art, Byzantine art as we envisage it would be inconceivable at any stage of its evolution, it cannot be said to have existed before Constantine founded that city (in 330) and the headquarters of the imperial government was transferred—theoretically at the same date—to the new capital. Theoretically, too, the art history of Constantinople begins in 330, when large-scale building was embarked on by the Emperor, and presumably the production of works of art began. But of Constantine's monuments, as of the other major works of the fourth and fifth centuries, exactly nothing has survived at Constantinople, except the ruined Basilica of Stoudion and the famous city walls (built in the fifth century). Thus our knowledge of the achievements of Byzantine art in the capital itself begins with such masterpieces as St Sophia, St Irene, and Sts Sergius and Bacchus, commissioned by Justinian and Theodora and dated to the middle of the sixth century. Other sixth-century works were the earliest wall mosaics at Constantinople and the oldest extant illuminated manuscripts made by the craftsmen of Byzantium. But lamentably few examples of these works remain and, to make things worse, between the reign of Justinian and the ninth century (save for a few unimportant fragments of uncertain date) all trace of this art disappears once more.

Still, as already noted, though first-hand knowledge of the painting of the period we call Byzantine under the forms it took in the capital itself is ruled out, we can learn something about it from monuments in other parts of the Empire. Even outside Constantinople the number of paintings available is relatively small as compared with architecture in particular, and with the works of decorative sculpture, small-scale carvings (in marble, wood, stone and ivory), not to mention statuary, which have come down to us. However, as regards the fifth century, considerable portions of the mosaics have survived at Salonica, in St George's, in the church known as the Church of the Virgin "Acheiropoetos" (i.e. not made with hands), and in the Oratory of Christ Latomos. Also at Salonica mosaics of the sixth, seventh and eighth centuries can be seen in the churches of St Demetrios and St Sophia. Further north, in Thrace, the ruined sanctuary named the Red Church (near Philippopolis) contains sixth-century frescos, while in the basilica at Parenzo in Istria, on the Adriatic coast of the Balkan peninsula, there exists a group of admirable sixth-century church mosaics.

These are closely affiliated to the mosaics in the churches of Ravenna on the opposite shore of the Adriatic, where so many splendid fifth- and sixth-century wall mosaics can still be seen today: in the Mausoleum of Galla Placidia and the Orthodox Baptistery, fifth-century works; in Sant'Apollinare Nuovo, San Vitale, Sant'Apollinare in Classe, and the so-called Arian Baptistery, sixth-century works (with seventh-century additions in the In Classe basilica). At Naples, chief seaport of the west coast of Italy, and the neighboring towns of Campania (Capua Vetere, Nocera, Nola) and also at Albenga on the Ligurian coast there are some fine fifth-century mosaics in baptisteries and martyries. As already observed, the mosaic decorations of this period in the churches of Milan and Rome owe too much to purely local art traditions to call for mention here; exceptionally, however, the mosaics of the triumphal arch of Santa Maria Maggiore (432-440) have more affinities with contemporary works properly styled Byzantine in other Mediterranean lands. Later on, from the seventh to the ninth century, Greek and Levantine ecclesiastical authorities in these cities commissioned church paintings more or less in line with the art of Byzantium. This holds good, also, for a large part of the frescos in San Saba on the Aventine Hill and above all Santa Maria Antiqua in the Roman Forum (especially the seventh- and eighth-century frescos), and also for some murals in the Catacombs of Naples. In these Roman and Neapolitan works subsequent to the sixth century the Byzantine strains can be distinguished from the influences of local Italic tradition more clearly than in the earlier works; indeed we see here the beginnings of a parting of the ways, Latin on the one hand and Byzantine on the other (in the meaning assigned to the latter term from the ninth century onwards), between which hitherto it was less easy to discriminate.

Italy is the only one of all the Mediterranean lands in which a fairly large number of monuments have come down to us in good condition; as for the mural mosaics and paintings of the period from the fourth to the seventh century in countries that were for a long while (or still are) under Mohammedan rule, we have no satisfactory ocular evidence to go on. There can, however, be no doubt that painters dwelling in Asia Minor, Syria, the Holy Land and Egypt played an active part in the decoration of churches, since the most copious and detailed accounts we possess of paintings of this kind relate to churches in these areas. It was here that the themes of mural paintings were most diversified and artists most inventive; and this seems natural enough when we remember that from the fourth to the seventh century it was in these countries that Christendom, in all its manifestations, had its most active and influential centers. Whether we have in mind contemporary developments of "high theology" and the liturgy, or the beginnings of monasticism, the cult of relics and the great vogue of pilgrimages amongst all classes of the population, or the creative fervor that gave rise to the apocryphal writings and Christian iconography of the Holy Land—in all these fields we find that it was mainly in the lands east of Byzantium that the chief manifestations of these forms of Christian zeal took place—and in all alike art played an active part. It was also in the East that races with a long cultural tradition, though not so prosperous as they had been in the Empire's golden age, were anyhow immune from the invasions which, throughout this period, played havoc with Western Europe and its social and economic structure. A long-lasting peace and relatively widespread welfare certainly favored the activities set forth above and the progress of the arts of Christendom in the Byzantine East.

Thus it seems almost preposterous that, for the period from the fourth to the seventh century, all we should have to go on is the mosaic decoration of a single church, the Justinian basilica of Mount Sinai, which escaped destruction owing to the remoteness of the monastery and the Moslems' veneration of it; and (apart from a few fragments) two painted apses, frankly rustic in conception, in Christian mausolea of that faraway region, the Great Oasis of Egypt. However, in support of what the records have to tell us, excavations in Palestine, Transjordania, Syria, North Mesopotamia and Egypt and town clearances made at Damascus have brought to light some fragments and groups of paintings of various kinds which testify, if indirectly, to the wide extension of this art in the eastern provinces of the Empire before the Moslem conquest. Sometimes, in houses and Christian sanctuaries—at Antioch especially—but also in Early Christian churches in Palestine and Transjordania, we find mosaic pavements of the pre-Byzantine and Byzantine epochs, and these are obviously projections as it were upon the floor, of paintings on vaults and ceilings. Or, again, as in Dura-Europos and Tuna-Hermopolis (Egypt), we find second- and third-century mural frescos of various kinds, prefiguring Byzantine painting. And, finally, in Ommiad palaces and mosques—whose builders owed much to the art of Byzantine Syria—there are painted walls that reflect more or less faithfully the last phase of the Byzantine painting of pre-Islamic Syria, that is to say sixth- and seventh-century art. A collation of the indirect evidence we gather from these sources with the decoration of a Christian church under the Ommiad jurisdiction (the eighth-century Bethlehem mosaics) confirms the fact that what we have styled the *koiné* of first-period Byzantine painting extended to the most easterly provinces of the Empire, and that large-scale monumental painting flourished in these regions.

We should probably have more evidence pointing in this direction, were it not for the total disappearance of the small objects of art adorned with painting which would have remedied the dearth of large-scale pictures, and which prove so helpful when we try to trace the course of Christian iconography or the ornamental arts, and even decorative sculpture. But, as regards the countries east of Byzantium, panel-paintings and illuminations of the period are almost as few and far between as mosaics and frescos, and the exact dates, and notably the provenance, of such few works as remain are often highly dubious—a circumstance which obviously detracts from their historical, if not from their artistic significance. Thus there is a small group of icons painted on wood in the wax (encaustic) technique, most of which have been discovered on Mount Sinai, or came from it (in the Treasury of Sinai, Kiev Museum and Santa Maria Nuova, Rome). These certainly throw light on the origins of that special kind of painting on wood which had such a remarkable flowering at Byzantium and, by way of Byzantium, in Russia after the ninth century. But the exact age of the Sinai icons is hard to fix, in view of the few points of comparison available and the rude craftsmanship of some. Their place of origin is equally uncertain, given the probability that Sinai served merely as a place of refuge for these icons as it did for some sixth-century mosaics. Quite possibly it was in Egypt rather than in Palestine that, under the form of icons, the technique and characteristics of the Roman portrait held their own the longest.

As for paintings in books, that is to say miniatures in illuminated manuscripts, only one is extant which undoubtedly was made in Constantinople (in the early sixth century). Unluckily for the student of Byzantine art, the vignettes in this book, a copy of the *Materia Medica* of Dioscorides, are merely replicas of Hellenistic illustrations prior to the founding of Constantinople—with one exception, the portrait of Julia Anicia, the noble Byzantine lady who commissioned this copy (dated to approximately 500 A. D.). Perhaps the Greek "Cottonian Genesis" also hailed from Constantinople; but only some charred fragments of this are extant (in the British Museum). Of outstanding interest are three fine illustrated books of high aesthetic value—the Vienna *Genesis*, the Rossano *Gospel Codex* and the "Sinope fragments" in the Bibliothèque Nationale, Paris. All have that purple ground whose high aesthetic qualities we shall deal with later, and, judging by the style, are sixth-century productions; we can but guess, however, at their provenance, nor can we be sure it was the same for all three books. True, it may well have been Constantinople, but this is mere conjecture. A few illuminated pages in other Greek manuscripts, also of an early date, complete this all-too-meager list, unless we—tentatively—include some series of miniatures belonging to this period but known to us only by way of ninth- and tenth-century copies or imitations (Psalters, the "Job" and "Joshua" Rolls). We are much farther from Byzantine art properly so called when we come to the miniatures in a fifth-century Chronicle of Alexandria, and those in a small group of Gospels in Syriac—to begin with the Florence Gospel, whose script is dated to 586. Here, anyhow, we have the advantage of being able to assign these works to specific localities (Egypt, Northern Mesopotamia); none the less this art, though confirming in a general way the extension of the *koinē* of the period as far as the banks of the Nile and the Upper Euphrates, does no more than illustrate certain local forms assumed by this artistic lingua franca and has very little to tell us about the painting in the great cities of the Near East.

Thus the indisputably Byzantine paintings known to us are too few to justify any definite conclusion as to the specific characteristics of Byzantine pictorial art in the period from the fourth to the seventh century. We can at most discern some of its aspects, those which were common to most Mediterranean painting of this period.

SECOND PERIOD

After the ninth century things are very different; the works of art available are both numerous and varied, their study is rewarding, and it is easy to distinguish in Byzantium itself, in the Near East and in Western Europe, local schools of painting, each pursuing a well-defined aesthetic trend peculiar to itself. This crystallization of specific idioms in several contemporary art centers was, it would seem, a slow and gradual process, which began in the sixth and seventh centuries. (In this context reference may be made to what was said above as to Roman frescos; this holds good for Coptic painting, which at a very early stage detached itself from the parent stem

—the art of classical Antiquity—, and also for Armenian painting, which followed closely in its wake. This emancipation was yet more pronounced in Irish painting, which in any case was less concerned with Mediterranean traditions.) In the eighth and ninth centuries the brief flowering of Carolingian painting, even in its imitations of ancient works, and despite the variety of styles practiced by its guilds of craftsmen, was from start to finish quite different from that of the Byzantines; nor have we the slightest trouble in distinguishing between them. From now on the gulf between Byzantine and Latin artists rapidly widened; whenever in the tenth century the Ottonian painters assimilated a Byzantine prototype, they changed it out of recognition, and by the twelfth century Romanesque aesthetic was employing a repertory of forms so rigidly defined that when attempts were made (e.g. in the Rhineland) to imitate contemporary Byzantine paintings, these merely brought into greater prominence the divergencies of Romanesque procedures. The gap between Byzantine and Latin art tended to widen as time went by, and when the Gothic age ensued in Western Europe its painting embodied so many recent and significant discoveries of the Latin art world that contemporary Byzantine painting (unvarying in its basic principles) had the air of a survival from a bygone age. This time-lag had a curious effect; it enabled Italian thirteenth- and fourteenth-century painters to link up for a moment with the Byzantines and make important borrowings from them. Like the humanists of a somewhat later period, they extracted from this conservative art its residue of classical Antiquity; for though artists had now before their eyes the ancient sculpture recently unearthed in Italy, they had nothing as yet to go on as regards the painting of the ancient world. Thus it was only in Italy, and in the twelfth and thirteenth centuries, that more or less active intercourse developed between Byzantine art in the strict sense and the native art of the Latin peoples.

In the East the line of demarcation is no less clearly definable than in the West. Of the Christian arts which had flourished hitherto in Asia little remained after the Arab conquest; the work produced in lands ruled by the Mohammedans, in Egypt and Mesopotamia, has an aesthetic utterly different from the Byzantine. For there, too, as in Europe, the Mediterranean artistic *koinē* of the past was translated into the local languages, all the more unlike the idiom current in Byzantium in that Greek influences in Asia were countered by an ascendancy of Islamic arts, Arab and Persian. The only non-Moslem arts that held their ground effectively were those existing on the periphery of the Mohammedan world, in Armenia and Georgia. The evolution of mediaeval Armenian art proceeded on much the same lines as that of Byzantine (this is especially true of Armenian painting); in both we find a similar handling of stock themes and motifs appertaining to the artistic *koinē* of the close of Antiquity, and moreover their activities ran parallel in time. However, though the repertory was the same, the Greeks and Armenians almost always gave it quite different aesthetic interpretations; thus it is relatively easy to distinguish between their respective outputs.

The position of Byzantine art as regards the art of the Georgians was similar, but with a slight difference due to the fact that, being of the same religious persuasion, the

Georgians could borrow more freely and easily from the Byzantines. In a far greater measure this dependence on Byzantine art made itself felt in the painting of the countries inhabited by Orthodox Slavs: Bulgarians, Serbians, Russians and (a little later) Rumanians. Indeed the painting in these countries stemmed directly from various trends of Byzantine art, with the result that the geographical frontiers of the latter are less distinct in these regions. But since in the Slav countries, especially in Russia and to a less extent in Rumania, no real emancipation from Byzantine art took place until after the fall of the Eastern Empire, the task of distinguishing between Byzantine paintings and Slav and Rumanian paintings is largely superfluous, unless we approach the subject from the angle of the local political and ethnical factors conditioning the evolution of the aesthetic of mediaeval art. From the purely aesthetic angle, all the painting of the Slavs and Rumanians, and up to a certain point that of the Georgians, remained Byzantine until the close of the Middle Ages, and underwent only very slight modifications in these countries. In fact the new artistic *koine* of the close of the Middle Ages throughout Eastern Europe was not only created in the first instance by Byzantium, but constantly replenished by Byzantium.

When after this general survey of mediaeval Byzantine painting we examine it more closely, we find that it falls into several categories. First there are the great wall mosaics, crowning achievement of Byzantine art throughout its course. A small number of these can be dated to the ninth and tenth centuries, but the majority belong to the eleventh, twelfth and fourteenth. Though the extant works represent but a tithe of the products of this prolific and long-lived art, we have the advantage of being able to see original works, not copies, and to feast our eyes on the masterpieces of artists resident in the capital and employed by the Emperors and connoisseurs of the day.

Alongside the mosaics, fresco painting was currently employed for the decoration of mediaeval Byzantine churches, and owing to its greater flexibility this medium gave the artist more scope for original creation. Judging by surviving fragments, the walls of the churches in Constantinople must often have been covered with paintings, but it is chiefly in the provinces and above all in countries to which Byzantine art had spread that the finest and most complete fresco sequences can be seen today. In faraway Cappadocia we find a long series in the most archaic style, while in Greece and Cyprus, in Serbia, Russia and Bulgaria rustic works in a purely local style are juxtaposed to superb paintings that reflect the twelfth- and thirteenth-century creations of the metropolis. In the following century this art made exceptionally rapid strides and dozens of churches with fresco cycles dating to this period still exist in Constantinople, Salonica, Mistra and Crete, and above all in the Slav countries. Numerically anyhow, these late murals—in the lineage of the monastery decorations of the period of the Turcocracy, on Mount Athos and elsewhere—constitute the bulk of Byzantine painting.

It is only in the manuscripts that we find a like abundance of paintings, but most of the illuminated Byzantine books and the finest works in this technique belong to an earlier period. Seemingly the illustrated manuscript came into fashion at Byzantium at the close of the ninth century and reached its apogee in the eleventh and twelfth centuries. To this period may be ascribed almost all the masterpieces of the Byzantine miniaturists and the best illustrations in a popular vein. Following the temporary domination of Constantinople by the Crusaders (1204 to 1261), the miniature, as being essentially a luxury art, fell into a decline; all the same many fine works of this kind were produced up to the mid-fourteenth century. Greek scribes had the regrettable habit of never noting down the place of origin of their manuscripts, and this complicates the problem of the historian when he seeks to ascertain their provenance. However, for various reasons, many of them can be assigned to Constantinople. Throughout the Middle Ages the ablest craftsmen worked for the Emperors in the capital and a fairly large number of illustrated books deriving from their *scriptoria* (certainly the best of the period) are extant. Others existed in the various monasteries of Constantinople and the neighborhood; also in Patmos, on Mount Athos and the Bithynian Mount Olympus. But the conditions under which these mediaeval provincial *scriptoria* functioned were quite different from those under which the Western illuminator worked; almost always, though in varying degrees, they were subject to the direct influence of the leading craftsmen's schools in the capital and of prototypes emanating from these. This indeed is what prevented the growth of autonomous local schools of Byzantine miniaturists on the lines of those in the West of Europe. On examining the picture sequences produced by the Byzantine illuminators we find that they bear less resemblance to the work of independent creative artists than to that of members of a family stemming from the same ancestor. This was only to be expected when we consider that the two distinctive features of Byzantine culture were, firstly, the centripetal structure of the monarchic state, its framework, and, secondly, the respect invariably accorded to traditions of the past. Unlike mural painting, the work of the illuminators found relatively little favor in the outlying countries into which the Byzantine aesthetic was diffused; and in any case the period of its diffusion in Eastern Europe synchronized more or less with the decadence of the miniature, even in the metropolis itself.

From the ninth century on, Byzantine religious sentiment fostered the development of panel-painting in the form of icons on wood. Probably the craftsmen's workshops specializing in this genre were located chiefly in the monasteries, but few Byzantine icons previous to the fourteenth century have survived, and it is only in the light of later works produced in Greek, Russian and other workshops that we can judge what the iconography and the prevailing forms of the earlier icons may have been. But here we must walk warily; conservative though it was, the art of the icon must certainly, like the other arts, have undergone considerable changes. When all is said and done, the aesthetic qualities of the icon can be effectively determined only in the light of works belonging to the end of the Byzantine period and especially Greek and Russian works subsequent to the Turkish conquest of Byzantium—which is why they are only briefly discussed in the present volume.

On the other hand we have included, tentatively, a few specimens of Byzantine enamels. Usually such work is ranked among "minor" or "applied" arts, but these epithets are pointless where Byzantine artists are concerned. After all, do not mosaics and illuminations—though unquestionably rating among the outstanding achievements of Byzantine art—fall, respectively, into the categories of "applied" and "minor" arts? The truth is that the Byzantines were particularly sensitive to the intrinsic beauty of the materials they handled, costly metals, polished marble and precious stones, and delighted in the novel and colorful effects obtained by juxtaposing them. In these so to speak "symphonic" works the painting proper is often associated with techniques which we are tempted to assimilate to goldsmiths' work (examples are two icons of the Archangel Michael in the Treasure of St Mark's at Venice); nevertheless, aesthetically all these elements form an organic whole. It should be noted in this connection that the modern notion that one species of art is inherently "superior" to another meant nothing to the Byzantines; they had a scale of values of their own, in which the costliness and rarity of the materials employed and the difficulties in manipulating them ranked high. All these conditions were eminently satisfied by enamel work, whose technique was probably mastered at Byzantium at an early date, and whose flowering synchronized with that of the de-luxe illuminated book (tenth to twelfth centuries). Its prestige was clearly bound up with polychromy in general, and above all with a prevailing taste for polychrome decoration employing several techniques simultaneously. By a judicious use of enamels for figures and ornamental details in the larger decorative works, together with inlays of gold and precious stones, the artist achieved a highly effective over-all integration of the composition. For enamel-work has this in common with the stained-glass window, with translucent cabochons and gold ornaments (as well as with mosaics), that the light striking through its surface is refracted at different angles and becomes amazingly "alive." Undoubtedly the sheen of the colors in enamel-work far surpasses that of ordinary painting, and in this respect enamel-work has the same aesthetic qualities as those of metals, glass and crystal. None the less the enamels may properly be included in the realm of Byzantine painting.

PROGRAMS BEFORE ICONOCLASM

The status assigned to art varies greatly from one cultural group to another. In Byzantium art was given a leading place; indeed it was in this field, more than in any other, that the Byzantine contribution to world culture found its fullest expression and showed the most originality. Needless to say, this does not mean that Byzantine painting was ever called on to depict the life of Byzantium; in fact, from the documentary angle, its value is but trifling. Its field of action lay elsewhere. What then was it that the Byzantine world asked of this art which it cultivated for so long a period? As usual, it is by examining the "programs" of the works of art produced that we can best determine its social function.

It is obvious that the countries and communities which we style Byzantine were at their inception and over a long period those of the ancient Roman Empire, and, subsequently, of its Eastern moiety. The functions there assigned to art seem to have been much the same as those obtaining before the transfer of the capital to the Bosporus, and so far as painting is concerned, we find that the taste for it was widely diffused, extending not only to the humblest ranks of society but to the remotest corners of the Empire. A great number of craftsmen's workshops catered for this vast public, more or less capable of appraising a work of art, who, following the fashion of the times, had their houses and mausolea decorated with frescos, the floors of private houses and public edifices with mosaics, and who also commissioned portraits. The repertory of these craftsmen (who were first and foremost decorators) included imitations of famous ancient pictures on literary, mythological or homiletic themes, and sometimes of a talismanic order. Though the copyists and their patrons were fully aware of the original significance of these subjects, they treated them with scant respect, sometimes as mere decorative motifs. In this repertory were some cycles of pictures which a little earlier had been inspired by living and active religions—for example the Dionysiac cycles—but these too were incorporated in the common stock of *motifs d'agrément* popularized by the new techniques of reproduction. Lastly, during the Early Period of Byzantine art one of the minor functions of pagan art, the illustration of scientific treatises, held its ground to some extent, since a great many schools of medicine, law and philosophy still flourished in the big towns of the Empire, where these illustrated manuals certainly found readers capable of appreciating them.

As employed in monumental decoration, this painting ventured beyond the strict confines of the pagan arts only when dealing with astrological or prophylactic themes. It usually figured in dwelling-houses or public buildings (*e.g.* Baths) and was doubtless to be seen at its most ornate and majestic in the great public edifices built by the emperors and in the "Sacred Palace" of the sovereigns themselves. But of all this splendor little has survived except some mosaic pavements, the best of which are at Antioch and in the Great Palace at Byzantium. None of these works is later than the sixth century, but we may be sure that this non-religious art continued to exist at Constantinople in the Middle Ages. Still, as we shall see, its program must have undergone a progressive shrinkage.

It was in the Palace of the Emperors that, from the early days of the Roman Empire, an unashamedly pagan art, intended purely for the pleasure of the eye and to create an atmosphere of luxury, flourished alongside a propagandist art based on the theory of "the divinity that doth hedge a king" and serving the interests of the ruling House. The programs sponsored by this official art were as precisely defined as the ends to which it was applied, and owing to the wide diffusion ensured it by all-powerful monarchs, this propagandist art had come, even before Constantine, to bulk large in the artistic output of the age. Located at the very heart of the Empire and therefore easily controllable, it was eminently a "directed" art, its directives issuing from the throne itself and, having learnt from long experience the best methods of expressing certain elementary ideas (e.g. victory and power) that appealed to the masses, was well equipped for the Empire-wide propaganda that was required of it. All forms of art were enlisted in the service of this "imperial idea." In painting it found expression in mural frescos and mosaics, paintings on wood and on canvas, and it crept into the illustrated books. Both the cycles of pictures and individual pictures in all these groups can be differentiated from similar productions of the pagan past and should be assimilated, rather, to religious art, since they too were called on to bear witness, and served doctrinal ends.

But, with the triumph of Constantine, a new patron of the arts came on the scene and rapidly took precedence of all others, such was the scope of its artistic activities and the geographical area they covered. This new patron was the Christian Church, which Constantine's initial support and subsequent imperial edicts placed in a highly favorable position for intervening in the artistic evolution of the Empire—and even, perhaps, *obliged* it thus to intervene, given the fact that in the Roman world it was taken for granted that any art in the grand manner should "represent" the important institutions of the day and keep them in the public eye. Hitherto the Church had paid little heed to art, but now the Church Triumphant felt called on to provide itself with an architecture and iconographical system worthy of its new eminence, and to draw up the first Christian repertories which, from the fourth century onward, were added to those of pagan and imperial art (described above) and very soon thrust them into the background. Endowed with copious funds provided by the imperial government and the rulers themselves, the Church made an entrance into the field of art that was all the more spectacular in that she had started from nothing or next to nothing. For, in the first centuries of the Christian era, it was almost always private individuals who commissioned the decorations of their tombs; though it is possible that from the third century onward, the ecclesiastical authorities in Rome as in the East (at Dura, for example) sometimes took the initiative in enlisting the services of artists.

Thus naturally enough the Church authorities, when faced by the necessity of creating a great Christian art that neither the Gospels nor the early Fathers of the Church had contemplated, accepted guidance from the art around them. True, their aim was to extract from heathen art all that might be used for the advancement of the Christian Faith, its prestige and the grandeur of its ritual; nevertheless of the many methods by which this might have been done (and by which it was subsequently done) they selected only a few, those which best accorded with the feelings of all devout believers after the triumph of Christianity in the Empire, and also with the methods currently adopted by officially sponsored forms of art whose mission it was to shore up and to propagate an ideology.

Thus a program was drawn up which, though not exclusive, was followed more or less invariably for several centuries and in which (as in all countries at the close of Antiquity) painting played a leading part. Painters were called on to decorate the interiors and sometimes the façades of churches. Other sacred edifices, martyries and baptisteries, were adorned in the same way; in fact these decorations may have slightly preceded those of the places intended for eucharistic reunions, that is to say the churches. Moreover painting was still lavishly employed in the Christian mausolea. In the fifth century (if not earlier) painting made its first appearance in Christian books, shortly after the portraits, done from the life or retrospective, of saintly personages, heroes of the Faith, painted on veils or panels. Meanwhile, in all the various kinds of Christian monumental painting, purely decorative elements predominated; sometimes their sole function was that of embellishing the "House of God" and its outbuildings on the same lines as the palaces, using the same techniques and producing a similar effect of sumptuous display. It was in fact from the Imperial Palace and an art enlisted in the service of the divine emperor that the big mosaics in the churches drew inspiration for the apses and the "triumphal" arches in which an effigy of God loomed large, invested with the temporal majesty of the deified monarch. To start with, only a vision of God in his celestial abode figured on the wall behind the altar. In the sixth century, however, with the enlargement of the choir, scenes and historical figures to which a eucharistic symbolism was imparted were represented, while on the walls of the nave, besides the purely iconographic decorations, were depicted selected episodes (their range was limited) from the Old or the New Testament, or both together. Despite the persistence of allegorical motifs (the Lamb of God and sheep) and symbolic devices (the cross and monogram of Christ), much recourse was had to Bible stories. These historical pictures may be assimilated to the quotations from the Old Testament and Gospels so frequently employed in sermons and the liturgy; while, in their general appearance, the compositions in the apses have a literary parallel in the emperors' triumphal panegyrics.

While deriving from funerary art, the picture sequences in baptisteries provide the earliest examples of a *rapprochement* between historical scenes and abstract patterns serving as iconographic counterparts of the liturgy, and in them we find the first symbolical interpretations of the functions of places of worship. Whereas the picture sequences in the martyries (shrines for the cult of holy relics) stemmed from the age-old traditions of the Christian tombs. Subsequently, above all in the East, the martyries approximated more closely to ordinary churches and their depictions of the scenes basic to man's salvation (that is to say episodes from the Gospel narrative, notably Christ's Birth, Passion and Resurrection) prepared the way for the church decorations of a later period.

Though there is no conclusive evidence, it would seem that this monumental art, which spread over the whole of Christendom between the fourth and sixth centuries, originated chiefly in Rome and Palestine, and that Byzantium did no more than adopt and propagate it. It is particularly difficult to trace the origins of those specific forms of this art which seem unlikely to have derived from the great centers of the Empire, and also have no clear association with the Holy Places of Palestine. The paintings in the martyries and tombs during the Byzantine era probably carried on local traditions which were perhaps anterior to Constantine. Likewise the picture cycles based on apocryphal anecdotes of the lives of Christ and the saints may also have reflected local cults beyond the control of the central ecclesiastical hierarchy. Seemingly, however, it was in Palestine that they were given their iconographical interpretation, and thus, as regards their origins, they link up with the most "official" and ubiquitous Gospel themes (e.g. the Women at the Tomb and the Ascension).

Only very rarely do we find pictures motivated by spontaneous personal piety, as against paintings of time-honored types. Nevertheless some pictures of this kind exist; these are the *ex-voto* works whose more or less simple iconographical content is usually of a personal order (mosaics at St Demetrios of Salonica, frescos at Santa Maria Antiqua and on the wall of an "hagiasma" at Salamis in Cyprus).

Being more fragile than the buildings, the early Byzantine painting was now so thoroughly obliterated everywhere that the few, widely scattered specimens available fail clearly to reflect the territorial shrinkage of the Empire after the Arab conquests in the seventh century and those of the Seljuks in the eleventh. But the fact must not be blinked that, from the middle of the seventh century on, Egypt and Syria were no longer provinces of the Empire, nor dominated by the art prevailing in it. The "dark ages" of Byzantium were beginning and, from the viewpoint of Byzantine art history, they lasted for over two centuries—from Heraclius (611-641) to Justinian II (685-711) —the period of the terrible wars with Islam, the Slavs and the Bulgarians. Then, from Leo III (717-741) to Theophilus (829-842), came the period of Iconoclast domination. True, the art of painting never died out completely at Byzantium; it was only the depiction of sacred figures that the Iconoclast ban on "imaging" brought to an end. But all the works of that period have disappeared, some owing to the zeal of the Iconoclasts, and the rest (those with which these "heretics" replaced them) owing to that of their adversaries, who triumphed in 843.

Thus we know very little of the course of painting in this period. It would seem, however—judging by the few fragments of mosaics (St Demetrios at Salonica) and of frescos (Greek works at Santa Maria Antiqua and San Saba in Rome) which have survived—that the lay-out of church decorations changed a good deal in this obscure period between the age of Justinian and that of the Iconoclasts. Votive pictures proliferated on church walls as independent units, thus obscuring or obliterating the notion of wall decoration as an organic whole, and, by the same token, extended the use of sacred iconography to monumental painting. To this period may probably be assigned the first church decorations composed of religious scenes placed end to end: some depicting Gospel incidents, others (the great majority) saints, episodes in their legends and services rendered by them to individual Christians.

It was probably these iconographic miscellanies that the Iconoclasts objected to above all. But instead of replacing them with plain monochrome surfaces (as in Protestant churches and Moslem mosques), they replaced them with another species of paintings, which likewise had its "program": that of the secular art of the palaces, which (as we have seen) comprised elements of the monarchic cycle (examples of which could be seen in the eighth century in the Palace of Constantinople) and also the paintings, very similar in composition, with which Ommiad Mohammedan princes had recently adorned their new residences, to such brilliant effect.

PROGRAMS AFTER THE PASSING OF ICONOCLASM

The return to religious imagery after a bitter conflict brought more than a mere resumption of the *status quo*; the Church Triumphant declared officially (and this was a new departure) that effigies of Christ and the saints contained a spark of the "divine energy" and that their contemplation was beneficial to the soul. Invested with this religious function, pictures of sacred subjects soon cast into the shade all others, and came to reflect in their style their assimilation (henceforth definitive at Byzantium) to sacred objects. And in the period following Iconoclasm their style underwent certain changes due to the same cause: the attribution by the Church of an enhanced religious value to the work of art.

The end of the ninth century saw the appearance of the first church decorations of a type that was to persist, under varying aspects, until the close of the Middle Ages. The "New Church" founded and decorated by the Emperor Basil I in the precincts of his Palace was famous in its day and was perhaps the earliest example of this art; or, more precisely, its earliest notable example—since innovations affecting both art and religion often begin by figuring in little known works, and the Emperors may well have been chary of innovations that had not already been tried out. This kind of decoration was planned for cube-shaped churches with a central dome. And just as these were conceived of as microcosms, small-scale reproductions of the Cosmos, so the pictures on the walls and vaults were laid out on a systematic plan for the instruction of the worshippers. In the dome and its substructure were shown the holiest figures of the world invisible; in the choir, the sacred mysteries pertaining to the same world made intelligible; in secondary vaults and on straight walls, the events of Christ's life on earth, corresponding to the various stages of man's redemption, to which the Masses solemnized in the church bore constant witness. This iconographic illustration of the Mass formed part of a plastic rendering of the Ideal Universe and corresponded to a notion cherished by the Byzantines—that the liturgy of the Church was but an earthly counterpart of the never-ending Mass solemnized in heaven by the angels, who, only after the redemption of mankind by the Word made Flesh, could make its nature known to man. Thus the Gospel cycles figuring in mediaeval Byzantine churches were reminders of man's return to union with God and the right he had regained to a place in God's Universe, as pictured in each church.

The typical picture cycle, laid out in terms of mosaic decoration which never came down to the ground but stopped short at a plinth of varying height, always followed a well-balanced compositional scheme, as may be seen in the Chapel of San Zeno in Santa Prassede, Rome (early ninth century); the central nave of St Sophia, Constantinople (after 900): an early variant in which the Gospel scenes are few or absent; the "Nea" of Basil I; another Constantinopolitan church decorated in the time of his son Leo VI; St Luke's in Phocis; the "Nea Moni" of Chios and the church at Daphni—an amplified variant including the Gospel cycle. In fresco decorations the marble-faced socle is absent and replaced by rows of saints, the Gospel scenes being intercalated between two zones allotted to the saints (the earliest examples are eleventh- and twelfth-century churches in Cappadocia). Even before the Byzantine period, there had been a long-standing practice of aligning portraits of saints and the dead along the bases of the walls of tombs. In the Middle Ages this lay-out was retained for frescos, but departed from in the more sophisticated compositions in mosaic.

In the twelfth, and still more during the thirteenth and fourteenth centuries, sacred scenes figured in the decorations in even greater numbers: illustrations of Gospel episodes, and above all of Christ's Childhood and Passion, incidents in saints' lives, subjects drawn from church calendars or Books of Hours, paintings inspired by the liturgy and eschatological themes. Here we have, in part, a return to the most ancient formulas (hagiographic sequences and the cycles of Christ's Childhood); indeed it would seem that the highly sober, schematic decorations of the ninth, tenth and eleventh centuries had never wholly broken with the descriptive, pedagogic monumental paintings of the long picture cycles of the past; these being reproduced in more traditionalist paintings and, perhaps above all, in the outlying regions of the Empire (e.g. some of the Cappadocian decorations). But it is clear that under the early Palaeologi Byzantine artists enlarged the field of the mural narrative picture in churches, chiefly by drawing on the iconographic repertory of the illuminated book, and that this change linked up with a certain relaxation (end twelfth-beginning fourteenth century) of the uniform control by the Church which was set up in the ninth century after the defeat of the Iconoclasts and in pursuance of the edicts of the last Oecumenical Council (787), when the dogma of the sanctity of icons was enounced. Strict control was not again enforced, it seems, until about the mid-fourteenth century, when the conservative-minded, rigorist monks known as Hesychasts gained the upper hand at Byzantium. Meanwhile the narrative picture cycles, of which there were now a great many, were developing a language that the plain man understood more easily than the laconic imagings of the tenth and eleventh centuries. For in its last phase Byzantine art underwent a sort of democratization, analogous to that of the early Byzantine period. Moreover the humanist tendencies and leanings towards realism evinced by certain painters at the beginning of this period may well have encouraged them to draw inspiration from the paintings of the close of Antiquity which (as in the illuminations in the Vienna *Genesis*) often illustrated a story at some length, in sequences of pictures placed side by side. Lastly, the tendency of Byzantine monumental painting towards the depiction of subjects in narrative form cannot be dissociated from the similar tendency evident in Italian frescos of the same period. This parallelism implies contacts, but it is not easy to say what form these took, though the historical conditions of the age (Greeks and Italians often living side by side) must have promoted them.

During the Middle Ages there was a demand for paintings on wood, illustrations and ornaments in manuscripts, and imaging done in enamel on metal grounds. All these types of portable paintings had flourished at Byzantium in an earlier epoch, but (with very rare exceptions) the only works that have come down to us belong to the Middle

Ages. Thus it is hard to say whether these forms of art progressed or declined in quality after the iconoclastic interlude, as against the period previous to it. In any case all alike benefited when the Church gave its official benediction to Christian figurative art, and the illuminated manuscripts derived a special advantage (as will be shown below) from the ending of the "quarrel about images." But we may also note a fact of a more general order; this advantage applied to religious art alone, since non-religious art had never been involved in the dispute. Thus obviously, as a result of the condemnation of Iconoclasm, secular painting must have lost its privileged position, for the good reason that religious painting could now be practiced on a large scale and also perhaps because the heretical iconoclast régime had favored the programs of pagan art.

True, in the ninth century, under Basil I, and later under other Macedonian rulers and the Comneni, the palace authorities sometimes commissioned painted decorations for the imperial residences and portraits of the emperors, and likewise illustrations for medical, historical and scientific works. All the monumental decorations of this kind at Constantinople are lost, but Slav copies of the Byzantine Chronicles, and the fine manuscripts of Oppian's poem on *The Chase*, of Nicander's *Theriaca* (on snake-bites), and Apollonius Citiensis' *De Articulis* give us a fair idea of the range of non-religious subjects covered by the mediaeval Byzantine painter. Yet, since these are without exception would-be exact copies of first-century originals, they have very little (apart from copyists' vagaries) to tell us about the procedures of mediaeval Byzantine art. It was not in works of this order that the spirit of the age found expression; secular painting, both that bespoken by the emperors and (above all) that whose sole function was to give pleasure, had no longer the same qualities or the same scope as it had had in Justinian's age. Now that religious art was in the ascendant, secular painting, in its decadence, could only just hold its own in a few, strictly limited fields. For, during the Middle Ages, Byzantine painting was almost entirely dedicated to the service of God; indeed themes of Christian iconography worked their way even into the decorations of the Imperial Court. Practically the only paintings on wood at this time were icons, depicting Christ, the Virgin, Saints, biblical and other sacred subjects. And, finally, almost all the illustrated and illuminated books were Bibles, Gospels, Psalters, collections of sermons, hagiographical calendars *(synaxaria, menologia)* and liturgies.

Paintings in books form a little world apart. The illustrations of, say, an episode in Genesis or the Gospels are transposed from one manuscript to another without any, or with only the slightest, modification. Invariably the same passages are given a picture, while others never have one—and it is not only those which do not lend themselves to illustration that are not illustrated. The truth is that the methods of the illuminator were those of the scribe; both alike were, functionally, copyists. Thus it is only copies that have come down to us; never originals, ancestors of the various "families" of copies. True, we always find differences of treatment between these copies and, artistically speaking, each has mannerisms of its own. Nevertheless the program of these groups of small pictures—that is to say, their subjects and cycles— never or hardly ever varies. This is especially true of the books in daily use, the prototypes of whose illustrations (in one or several versions) had been created once for all in the early Middle Ages: the first five books of the Old Testament (Pentateuch), the Lectionaries (Gospels) and Psalters. Though we cannot be sure of this, it seems probable that, before the Iconoclast schism, the four Gospels and most of the canonical books of the Old Testament had been given detailed illustration, following the text in unbroken sequence. But, with the exception of the *Genesis*, only mediaeval examples of these works have survived; indeed it may be that the Gospels were not illustrated in a continuous manner until the eleventh century (examples exist at Florence, Biblioteca Laurenziana VI, 23, and at Paris, Bibliothèque Nationale, MS Grec 74)—with, obviously, the exception of certain famous episodes such as the Childhood of Christ, the miracle of Cana, of the man born blind, the palsied man etc., which had been illustrated in picture sequences even before the age of Justinian. Many of the illustrations were mere stop-gaps, that is to say reproductions of stock pictures that would fit in anywhere, which lazy painters intercalated between the real (and older) illustrations so as to give the illusion of a continuous cycle. This expedient, old as art itself, can be detected even in the finest Byzantine manuscript with a "frieze" of illustrations that has come down to us, the *Joshua Roll* (believed to be a mid-tenth century work) at the Vatican.

The mediaeval Byzantine illuminator rarely added anything new to the repertory of religious illustration; when the text he was required to deal with called for personal initiative, he turned the difficulty by falling back on quotations from the Bible contained in it and reproducing traditional illustrations of these passages. Or again, as in the Roll at the Patriarchate of Jerusalem, an eleventh-century liturgy, he illustrated the prayers of the Mass with Gospel scenes, since these conveyed the mystical significance of the rite. Even when, having no option to do otherwise, he invented pictures appropriate to the text, he used as his starting-off point previous compositions, changing only details. (This procedure by analogy is familiar to the philologist; it is thus new words are coined in all languages.) So rare are the exceptions to this rule—so far as the illustration of entire books is concerned—that the work of a twelfth-century painter who composed a large and partly new set of illustrations for a collection of sermons on the Virgin by Jacobus of Kokkinobaphos is of outstanding interest. Naturally enough he, too, fell back on time-honored formulas and archetypes, but he also ventured to add something of his own. Two replicas of this work, remarkable for its additions to the conventional repertory of the Byzantine painter, exist—one at the Vatican and the other in Paris—and both may well be by the artist's own hand.

However little inclined these painters were to extend their range of subjects (the doctrine of the inherent sanctity of the religious picture must have discouraged individual enterprise in this respect), they felt no such compunction about the presentation and disposition of their pictures on the manuscript page. In this domain the spirit of mediaeval Byzantine art makes its presence clearly felt, especially in that class of paintings on manuscripts (peculiar to the Middle Ages) in which the picture proper is integrated into a purely decorative lay-out. Nothing indeed is more typical of Byzantine art in the tenth, eleventh and twelfth centuries than this new development of painting, these compositions in which a small picture, its richly decorated frame, the small figures and ornaments in the margins of the page and the written text combine to produce the effect of an organic whole. Also, this type of composition restored to the repertory of Byzantine painting certain elements which the glorification of the icon after the downfall of Iconoclasm had expelled from monumental painting and, in a more general way, brought into discredit. Thus in the decorations of de-luxe illuminated books, fragments of the pagan repertory—exotic beasts, hunting scenes, fountains, gardens, frolicsome *putti*—found a last refuge. Was it thought that these reminiscences of paganism were less insidious when reduced to the scale of the miniature? Or was it because such books were made for connoisseurs, and so there was less risk of these questionable images coming under the eyes of the general public?

Probably other manifestations of this secular art might have been found in the work done by goldsmiths for private persons and especially in the enamels of the period (like those embellishing ivory and silver caskets made for non-religious purposes), but very few such works have survived. An eleventh-century diadem in the Budapest Museum—it was intended, I think, to be worn by a woman—bears this out; it shows two Eastern dancing-girls in a garden thronged with birds. But the analogy between the paintings in books and those in enamel is visible in other fields; these paintings were used as models also in monumental art. In both cases we find the same idea put into practice: of combining in one and the same composition small painted pictures (done in enamel in the case of goldsmiths' work) and passages decorated with neutral, non-religious motifs (including animals, existing or fabulous, and human figures). Characteristic of Byzantine pictorial art in the tenth and eleventh centuries, this manner persisted into the twelfth, but thereafter is rarely to be seen; only in really outstanding works. Thus it was that at the close of the Byzantine epoch, the repertory of painting in general was almost identical with that of the somewhat more highly developed but strictly religious cycles of pictures that were still being reproduced on the walls of churches, and also with the much less varied imagings on wooden icons, whose subjects, too, needless to say, were always of a religious order.

BYZANTINE AESTHETIC

The aesthetic merits of Byzantine art have been recognized only during the last fifty years or so; therein it shared the lot of all the arts of the close of Antiquity and the early Middle Ages. For it was not until vanguard artists of modern Europe had undermined our deeply rooted faith in the absolute supremacy of the traditional aesthetic which, by way of the Renaissance, derived from ancient Greece, that the eyes of art-lovers were opened to the aesthetic value of Romanesque and Byzantine works, interest being focused primarily on sculpture as regards the Romanesque creations and on paintings and mosaics as regards Byzantine art. In fact any definition of the aesthetic of Byzantine art is something of a problem if we are to avoid lapsing into purely subjective evaluations and opinions too patently reflecting the tastes and outlook of our time.

The historical survey given above has, we hope, made it clear that the great flowering of art to which we give the name "Byzantine" does not fall into the category of art movements confined to a single race or to any specific area. It is, rather, an art-form bound up with the existence for over a thousand years (from 330 to 1453) of a Christian Empire ruled from Constantinople and predominantly Greek. It was not in the imperial capital that the foundations of Byzantine aesthetic were laid, nor was it in Constantinople that it ceased to function after the fall of the Byzantine Empire. However it was the permanence of the central government that enabled this aesthetic to hold its ground for so many centuries, since throughout this period both Church and State, whose power was absolute, gave it their full support. The very circumstance of its exceptional duration played a part in shaping the aesthetic evolution of Byzantine art; for all methods of artistic expression are not equally suitable for an art whose function it is to perpetuate itself, without toying with the illusion that it is progressing—indeed repudiating the very idea of progress. Thus the central authority at Byzantium not only had the last word in determining the artists' "programs" but also controlled the aesthetic of the figural arts; above all, after it was enacted that religious images were to be venerated as sacred objects and, as such, came under the control, explicit or implicit, of the Church. This edict (formulated by the Oecumenical Council of 787) did not merely lower the prestige of secular painting; it also indicated the manner in which the artist was to handle religious themes—and these were in the vast majority.

In sum, the aesthetic of mediaeval Byzantine works of art was stamped by the taste of those who, within the Byzantine community, were its almost exclusive patrons: high dignitaries of the Empire, headed by the Emperor, and the abbots of great monasteries. The former favored the sumptuous style and the refinement agreeable to an élite; the others expected of the artist that vision of the Cosmos and mankind which unfolds itself to the inner eye of the ascetic visionary.

When we regard Byzantine art as a phase in the evolution of Mediterranean art, we imply that, in its inception, it took over most of the characteristics of the latter. For what distinguishes Byzantine from Mediterranean art in general is primarily its *interpretation* of these elements. Thus Byzantine paintings, in their general approach to the composition of a picture, the human figure, a scene or landscape, are a continuation of the Greek and Roman painting of the first century of our era. The Byzantines did not look to other countries for their models, nor did they invent a type of picture that would have struck artists of the times of Augustus and Trajan as unfamiliar. And this holds good not only for the first Byzantine artists, but for all Byzantine painters up to the fall of the Empire, and even later.

From the fifth century on, ornamental motifs of Persian origin are often present in Byzantine painting. But, before this, Greek and Latin artists too (in, for example, some Pompeian frescos) had indulged in similar borrowings from the Iranian repertory. Thus there was nothing revolutionary, or even new, in the Byzantines' commerce with Sassanian art. It merely became more persistent, more vital, than in the past.

Now that the Empire included within its frontiers lands and races that had art traditions of their own, and these were being less and less replaced by influences stemming from the great centers of Graeco-Latin art, indigenous arts, in Syria, Asia Minor, Africa and Gaul, were given more scope and only slightly or sporadically affected by Graeco-Latin aesthetic. This, in fact, was fused into local tastes and traditions. So even in Italy itself Greek classicism was tempered by forms of expression racy of the soil.

In the third century this flowering of provincial forms in art had become general all over the Empire. Thus when Byzantine painters blended elements of classical tradition with others foreign to it, this was no radical innovation as regards the course of art in the Mediterranean lands. True, Byzantine art to begin with was essentially an art sponsored by the government whose headquarters from 330 on was Constantinople, and as such cannot be assimilated to a "regional" art. But it is a matter of common knowledge that provincial influences had made themselves felt in works of even the most official order, even before the founding of Constantinople and in Rome itself (e.g. the sculpture on Constantine's Triumphal Arch of 315). And it well may be that when Constantinople became the capital of the Empire, its art, too, was strongly tinctured with that of the nearby lands of Asia Minor. In any case the divergencies from classical tradition manifested in Byzantine works, if thus accounted for, would have nothing exceptional about them, given the practices of the age, nor would they involve any break with Mediterranean tradition.

True, Byzantine art, especially Byzantine painting, was a new departure as regards the art preceding it in the same countries, but its originality did not lie in any wholesale rejection of the practices and forms of the earlier art, nor in the introduction of new elements. It merely carried a stage farther the disintegration of ancient art which had set in before Byzantium, and accentuated it by selecting and incorporating the anti-classical elements which already existed in the art of the period of transition. But above all—in so far as the works we style Byzantine at this early stage were those which were sponsored by the Government and Church—it laid down and stabilized for a considerable period a number of set rules and forms precisely corresponding to the art forms prevailing in the fourth century. This official consecration of the *status quo* probably averted a more radical break-up of classical aesthetic and its forms (we have only to observe their fate in Latin Europe after the downfall of the Western Empire between the fifth and eighth centuries); but, by the same token, it prevented a complete return to classical aesthetic. The most that was achieved in this direction at Byzantium during many centuries was a series of tentative, more or less felicitous efforts to imitate specific classical models. Even as early as the reign of Constantine, thereafter under Theodosius, and intermittently throughout the Middle Ages, there were revivals of this sort (miscalled "renaissances") which, anyhow, had the merit of promoting direct contacts with works of classical Antiquity and broadening the artists' horizons. Indeed these contacts (which were not peculiar to Byzantium) were always salutary, and helped to keep the technique of painting at a reasonably high level. For, paradoxically enough, though the triumph of Byzantine art after the founding of the Christian Empire spelt the end of classical art, the only means it ever found for rejuvenating its failing powers was to transfuse into itself some drops of the blood of the classical ancestors it repudiated. Nevertheless the Byzantine aesthetic which, from the historical angle, appears to be a sort of compromise between classical tradition and the new artistic aspirations of the last centuries of Antiquity, succeeded in building up with these elements a language that, though it could not meet all the possible demands of art, attained a quite remarkable expressive power in several art-forms.

To evaluate its merits, we must begin by analyzing the compromise it stands for and isolating the forms and procedures foreign to classical tradition implicit in it. There is no question that these anti-classical elements are of greatly varying import in Byzantine works, and the part, considerable or otherwise, that they play in any given work does not necessarily depend on its date. At all periods Byzantine painters were sufficiently familiar with ancient painting to be able to approximate their work aesthetically, whenever they wished to do so, to that of the painters of Antiquity. For there was always a certain flexibility in the "Byzantine compromise"; it allowed for varying dilutions of classical with non-classical elements. In each period and in the work of almost every artist or group of artists we find a different and distinctive balance struck between these factors; often indeed the aesthetic merit of a Byzantine work derives from the way with which, in the same picture, classical and non-classical forms are played off against each other. Sometimes the result is sublime—occasionally grotesque.

The various ways in which the painters solved this problem are illustrated in the present work. Thus in the *Good Shepherd* of the Mausoleum of Galla Placidia, the artist has merely retouched the art of antiquity, but in a manner that was to be carried much farther in other works. The picture is carefully constructed, with a central axis and symmetrical wings; taken individually, the living beings and objects are freely disposed in space, yet we can hardly say that the problem of the third dimension is solved in this picture taken as a whole. Despite the gap in the foreground, the action seems to take place on an almost flat surface, carried on into the gold ground above.

The accentuation, by new methods, of the forms of an ancient prototype, as we find it in the Mausoleum at Ravenna, imparts to this mosaic a majesty and power that were lacking in the pastoral scenes of Antiquity. This effect is heightened by the mosaicist's tendency to make the picture functional to the wall it covers.

This is a fifth-century work. In other mosaics of the same period we find more reluctance to depart from the practices and aesthetic of traditional Roman painting. In the small panels, for example, on the walls of the nave at Santa Maria Maggiore, Rome, Old Testament scenes are treated like illustrations of a manuscript. The mosaic-workers showed much skill in arranging their tiny polychrome cubes so as to produce passages of broken color, delicate gradations of tone, effects of aerial perspective. But on a triumphal arch in the same basilica we find mosaics in which new procedures are being tried out; there is an occasional use of clean-cut planes and patches of strong color; the artist has carefully thought out his composition, using axial lines and *points de repère*, and established an over-all pattern with which the figures and their attitudes are made to conform. There is little or no attempt at suggesting the third dimension, except in the case of individual objects and figures treated independently, or, in a few cases, groups of figures constituting an homogeneous spatial unit (e.g. the Child Jesus on His throne with two women beside Him). Elsewhere, complete confusion reigns as regards the distances between objects and figures (are those toy-towns distant from, or near, the persons placed beside them?), and their points of contact with the ground are not always clearly defined. Cast shadows (when such there are) fan out in all directions, for there is no question of using light coming from a uniform source as a means of locating the various details of the picture within a single spatial referent.

Byzantine miniatures (if not the mosaics) of the tenth, eleventh, and twelfth centuries are often reproductions of pictures in which the proportions of classical and anti-classical elements were much the same as in the fifth-century mosaic panels at Ravenna, Rome and Salonica; I have chiefly in mind those illustrations in Gospels and Psalters of this period whose "antique" air takes us by surprise, considering their date. But evidently this is merely a question of historical perspective; the interesting point is that eleventh-century Byzantine artists still had recourse to the aesthetic procedures of the fifth century. The truth is that the Byzantine miniaturists (unlike their fellow artists in other lands) rarely indulged in any sort of originality, and the reason for this is evident. A "directed" art like that of Byzantium encouraged innovations in, primarily, the kinds of works that reached the masses and quickened their religious emotions: mosaics, frescos, icons. In the illuminated manuscripts, on the other hand, made for the wealthy connoisseur and seen only by a favored few, novelties which might offend the patrons' conservative taste in art were obviously uncalled-for; feats of technical ingenuity and pleasing effects were the artist's *desiderata*. Thus it was in the illuminations that the style of Late Antiquity persisted longest.

Meanwhile, from the sixth century on, great mosaic artists were creating works far more emancipated as regards the Graeco-Roman aesthetic. Of the processions of male and female saints in Sant'Apollinare Nuovo hardly anything has survived beyond some scraps of drapery reminiscent of the togas worn by Roman officials. Enough, however, remains to show that these garments are treated less as clothing bodies than as forming part of an all-over rhythmic pattern in line and color, governing the entire lay-out of this splendid frieze. The theme of the judge clad in a toga had long been a cliché of Roman official art, the effigy of a Roman judge normally consisting of a vaguely particularized head affixed to a standardized body. Thus the sixth-century mosaic does not stand for any new retreat from individualism; rather, it shows that this retreat now achieved an adequate artistic expression, since in a world conceived in terms of an hierarchy, whether the imperial world on earth or the heavenly kingdom, it is his rank or function more than his personality that "places" the individual. And painting was called on to bring this out; the humble ready-made toga of the municipal senator is rendered as a flat expanse of lustrous white, sometimes edged with purple, patterned with a system of lines defining and traversing it—and sublimated into a thing of beauty. The brilliant colors spangling the vestments of the women in the company of the Elect, the gold and mauve, are intended to suggest the glorious recompense of a Christian life on earth. The striking homogeneity of forms and movements is another aesthetic means of expressing both the supramundane nature of the theme and the equality of the Elect in the sight of God. Pillar-like forms of men and virgins—the former whitely gleaming, the latter colorful—alternate with the pillar-like trunks of palm-trees, and all alike are caught up in the same movement, emphasized by the throbbing color of an emerald-green background. Thus an art of line and color, disregarding optical experience and the material aspects of nature, built up a world of its own, a reality which carried conviction to the observer.

At San Vitale we have a complement as it were of this procession of saints, and are shown instead the Emperor, the Empress and their retinue. A complement and also its model; for if the imperial court reflects the court of heaven this is because divine majesty can be visualized only in terms of that of earthly monarchs. The artist might have represented the stately procession of Justinian, Theodora, court officials, prelates, officers and ladies of the palace with the utmost realism—for the scene is located not in Paradise but on earth, in the city of Ravenna which he certainly knew well. But he did nothing of the sort. These depictions of imperial pageantry are as remote from material reality as were the cortèges of saints. The reality which here, exploiting all the resources of his medium, the mosaicist has bodied forth might be defined as follows (stress being laid on the words in italics): the *Divine Emperor* and *Divine Augusta* are making the ritual offering incumbent on them, as *Christian Sovereigns*, to Saint Vitale. The artist has kept strictly to essentials, to the exclusion of all else. And one of the essentials (to the contemporary mind) was the divine nature of the rulers and the sanctity of their ritual acts. Thus it was the artist's duty to reproduce the *ordo* of the ceremony (even if, as is probable in the present case, it never actually took place) and to depict the members of the imperial retinue whose presence that *ordo* called for, each in the position assigned him by his rank and wearing the appropriate insignia. Scenes of this kind were pictorial equivalents of Deeds of Gift (Donations); thus it was needful to include, at the prescribed place and iconographically, everything that vouched for their authenticity. Hence the extreme care taken in the rendering of minute details of uniforms and the attributes of each court officer; hence, too, on the purely aesthetic plane, the artist's brilliantly successful use of subtle color effects (for example in the costumes of Theodora and her attendant ladies) so as to stress the outward splendor of the sovereigns and thus, by implication, their immanent divinity. By the same token, all that a ceremony of this order had in common with an ordinary imperial cortège was ruled out; and, to emphasize this discrepancy from reality, the artist deliberately "dematerialized" his personages; all have precisely the same height, the same breadth of shoulders, and all alike gaze straight in front, with a fixed, almost cataleptic stare. The bodies have no weight or substance, and seem to float in air, just off the ground. But for the fact that the faces of the leading figures are portraits, these might be styled symbolic pictures representing with consummate art, and in a transcendental ambiance, a ceremonial act performed by God's vicegerent on earth. The portrait-heads are pictographic "signatures" to this legal conveyance drawn up in terms of art.

The aesthetic of pictures of this type is characterized not only by the artist's minute attention to details (regarded as symbols of non-material values) but also by a lavish use of costly metals: gold and silver, crystal, precious stones, marble, porphyry and mother-of-pearl. Mural revetments in polychrome marble and incrustations of the materials named above are given a large place in all mosaic decorations, especially those of the fifth and sixth centuries. The portable paintings, enriched with goldsmiths' work, cabochons and enamels, testify to the same taste. Here not merely symbols are involved; generally speaking, the purely aesthetic effects produced by the employment of these glowing, translucent, highly polished surfaces cannot be wholly dissociated from the observer's consciousness of their costliness and rarity. And inevitably, during the Byzantine epoch, these sumptuous adornments conjured up thoughts of the glories of the "Sacred Palace" on earth and its celestial counterpart, God's dwelling. At first sight the "materialism" suggested by this predilection for costly substances may surprise us, considering the lofty, otherworldly aspirations of Byzantine art. But the ideas behind the lavish use of precious metals and porphyry were the same as those behind the realism of material details in even the most transcendental large-scale compositions (e.g. the Ravenna mosaics). Both alike were means of rendering more "tangible" to the spectator's imagination the supramundane reality he was invited to contemplate; the flawless imaging of a gold fibula or a piece of green porphyry inlaid with ivory was the vehicle of an initiation into a world supernal, and none the less intelligible. Indeed, do not the great mystics, in describing their loftiest visions, often have recourse to terms no less directly borrowed from aspects of earthly life?

These were not the only procedures used by the Byzantine artist for expressing the invisible. Thus, for example, while concentrating more and more on the portrayal of the human figure, he usually gave it a severely frontal pose, with the result that, as in the San Vitale mosaic, the eyes seem fixed intently on those of the spectator. Often the figure (ostensibly a portrait) is isolated; but sometimes it is alongside others, which, though similar, are not interrelated. Though Byzantine artists rarely troubled themselves about the relations between the real sizes of figures and objects, they frequently magnified the leading figure; thus Christ or the Emperor is at least a head taller than those beside him. An altar is as large as the church that houses it; the hand of a saint making the gesture of benediction is the same size as his head. A figure standing in the extreme foreground could, by leaning back, touch another figure coming up from behind a mountain rim. Care is taken that no part of the leading figures should be obscured by intervening persons or objects; they are depicted full length and well in view. Even a landscape of mountains or buildings is arranged in such a manner as to show off the figures to the best advantage. What, in fact, the artist is aiming at is not a faithful image but a tendentious interpretation of nature, adjusted to a preconceived scale of values which the observer is asked to take for granted. Nevertheless, to make this acquiescence a foregone conclusion, so to speak, he employs all the resources of his art; thus the over-size figure is placed plumb in the center, and forms the apex of a perfectly proportioned triangle; tiny trees are disposed in a series of curves, balancing, it may be, the outline of a stooping figure; the eye accepts a Lilliputian town on the right or left, because a larger patch of white at that point would impair the composition; the linear arabesque forms part of a schema that ignores the third dimension—thus a figure may be in two planes at once, e.g. partly in front of a mountain and partly behind it.

All Byzantine painters, even the mediaeval miniaturists most faithful to Hellenistic models, accepted the conventions, and also most of the procedures, of this somewhat intellectualist conception of art. We can gauge the hold these ideas had on them by the blunders they sometimes made when copying models executed in the classical manner, that is to say in terms of real optical experience. Nevertheless it is only the inferior works that give this impression of clumsiness due to the artist's vacillation between the ancient manner and the Byzantine. By and large—from the earliest mosaics at Ravenna and Salonica, and the oldest miniatures (the Vienna *Genesis*) onwards—we have no trouble in accepting the Byzantine compromise on its own terms; such is its expressive power and the splendor of its achievement.

The same characteristics may be found in Byzantine art of the Middle Ages, but before dealing with this, it may be well to point out at this stage that as regards most of their aesthetic conceptions and procedures the Byzantines cannot claim to have been pioneers. Whatever may have been the ultimate origin of this aesthetic (regarding which there is still much difference of opinion), one thing is certain: that it was adumbrated and indeed put into practice to some extent in the second- and third-century frescos at Dura-Europos on the Euphrates (Temple of the Palmyrene Gods and Synagogue) and at Tuna-Hermopolis in Egypt (a pagan mausoleum)—to mention only those sets of paintings in which what we have named "the Byzantine compromise" between a classicizing tradition and new tendencies is most in evidence. In many mosaic pavements, at Antioch, Naples ("Academy of Plato") and elsewhere, there are signs of the same trend, but in a less pronounced form. Already indeed in these works immediately preceding the Byzantine flowering we can trace starting-points of the various forms taken by Byzantine art, some—the monumental paintings—breaking more frankly with classical tradition, others—above all the illuminations—keeping closer to it.

When we use the term "classical" in this context, we are far from thinking of the art of the times of Pericles or Alexander; what we have in mind is the *koinē* of Graeco-Latin art during the imperial period prior to Constantine. In this, especially in the painting, Latin elements played a large part. But when we pass from essentially decorative murals to figure and landscape paintings, such examples of the latter as are dated to the later imperial period show an almost complete fusion of Greek and Latin idioms. In fact all painters worked everywhere on the same lines—except in outlying areas, the Euphrates area for example; though there, too, at Dura, paintings that link up with the style prevailing in the interior of the Empire (e.g. the frescos in the Christian Baptistery) are found alongside works in a distinctively local style. This explains why the classical elements retained by the artists of Ravenna, Constantinople and Antioch were more or less the same.

More specific (and of a later date as regards the art within the Empire) were the elements which, both before the rise of Byzantium, and thereafter in Byzantium, brought about a transformation in the aesthetic practice of the Mediterranean peoples.

Fifty years ago it was thought that the origin of the Byzantine style could be traced to the "illusionist" Italic painting (i.e. painting giving the semblance of reality) during the imperial epoch. Actually, however, the art which flourished in the first centuries of the Empire affected only the more classical types of Byzantine painting, notably the illuminations with their landscapes of hills and graceful edifices, their personifications of rivers and the facile charm of their draped figures. If we wish to trace the sources of the most powerful and original Byzantine creations (mosaics, frescos, icons) we must turn again to the murals at Dura. For the processions of sacrificial priests in the Temple of the Palmyrene Gods were beyond all doubt prototypes of the processions in Sant'Apollinare Nuovo and San Vitale. In both are many classical motifs, but handled on very different lines; we find flattened figures with strongly marked outlines, isocephaly (all heads on a level), bodies without weight or substance, space reduced to a minimum, figures turning their heads towards the spectator as they move past—in a word, an expressive art that does not seek to imitate what the eye sees or give the illusion of material reality. Noteworthy at Dura (as at Ravenna and other art centers) is the curious combination of an abstract over-all pattern with portrait heads and realistic details in garments and accessories. Affinities of another kind can be traced between Byzantine paintings and the Synagogue frescos: a decorative lay-out consisting exclusively of scenes arranged in self-contained historical sequences and inculcating religious truths; pictures with figures and buildings existing in an abstract space, relative sizes and positions being determined solely by a spiritual hierarchy.

Though its precise origin is unknown, the art of the Dura paintings suggests a blend of Hellenistic tradition with Iranian influences (the first-century reliefs in the Temple of Bel at Palmyra and other Syrian sculpture of the beginning of the Christian era can be traced to a similar source). In any case this art bears the stamp of the Semitic and Iranian East, and we learn from it a fact of capital importance: that there flourished in the second and third centuries in Syria a type of monumental painting that foreshadowed the Byzantine aesthetic of the sixth century and, also, various specific procedures subsequently employed by Byzantine artists under Justinian. True, we are not as yet in a position to demonstrate any more direct affiliation between these art manifestations so widely separated in time and space. But this much is certain: that amongst the paintings previous to Byzantium it is the frescos of the Syrian hinterland that above all point the way to the Byzantine aesthetic under its most original aspects, though not under those which maintained the illusionist style of the first centuries of our era. For despite their early date these Dura frescos already show a break—as at a later date Byzantine monumental paintings were to do—with two basic principles of illusionist painting: fidelity to the traditional suavity of classical art, and a will to imitate what the eye perceives.

We know nothing of the circumstances under which the new procedures invented by the Syrians (and other similar innovations) found their way into the studio-workshops of painters and mosaic-makers in the capitals of the Empire before and after Constantine, and a parallel study of contemporary sculpture throws little light on the problem. Antioch seems unlikely to have been the connecting link, now that a great many mosaic pavements have been discovered in that city which have nothing in common with the art of Dura. Should we, then, decide for Jerusalem and Constantinople? Actually, however, it may be that there is no "geographical" answer to the problem and that this art was taken over by certain Mediterranean peoples for a purpose or purposes other than aesthetic. Be this as it may, the methods of an exotic art would not have been accepted in the heart of the Empire, had they not found a favorable soil there; that is to say people who, by reason of their origins or religious beliefs, preferred the expressive language of the Near East to the traditional Graeco-Roman aesthetic; and other, highly placed persons who had the wit to realize that an anti-classical art of this sort would be a more suitable vehicle of political and Christian propaganda. Only one man is known to us as sponsoring this psychological attitude and predisposed to welcome the new art; and that is the great philosopher-mystic Plotinus. Whether or not he personally contributed to introducing the new aesthetic or fostering its growth within the ambit of Imperial art, he must certainly have been acquainted with its early ventures and realized what it was aiming at. For his *Enneads* are, in effect, a justification of this way of seeing Nature which, while disregarding the outward aspects of things and beings, claims to discern their very essences, and to establish contact with the "inner eye" of the beholder. And it was, again, Plotinus who believed in the possibility of discarding the analytical, discursive approach to knowledge and attaining it intuitively and completely by direct perception of the transcendent essence immanent in all matter. He even suggested specific procedures tending to this "dematerialization" of reality, traces of which can seemingly be found in the art of Late Antiquity; suppression of the space dimension, of foreshortening, of physical light, of perspective, of an horizon line determined by the spectator's point of sight, and so forth. Thus the ideas of Plotinus were adopted by the artists; material objects became transparent both *inter se* and to the mind's eye, enabling the latter to discern those spiritual values which are the one authentic reality and, as such, the only proper study for the philosopher—and for the artist. Obviously such theories would appeal not only to devotees of mystical religions and to the Christians, but also to the upholders of the divine right of the emperors, when they sought methods of expressing the mystical basis of this doctrine in terms of art. Assuming this was so, we can now see what it was that led to the relinquishment of classical aesthetic, so obviously unfitted to serve such ends, and the adoption of the new art and anti-classical forms sponsored by Near-Eastern artists.

In the first half of the seventh century some remarkably fine goldsmiths' work was produced at Constantinople, in the form of imitations of bas-reliefs with mythological subjects going back to the first centuries of our era. This taste for the plastic forms of Antiquity seems to have been widespread; we find it also in contemporary frescos made by Greeks at Santa Maria Antiqua in Rome. Thus the archangel's head here reproduced, another archangel (in the Annunciation), St Anne, the Descent into Limbo and St Demetrios are excellent examples of this kind of Byzantine painting, which, though following the art tradition of the San Vitale mosaics, comes perhaps closer to the ancient Greek aesthetic. Striking features of these works are the careful modeling of bodies and faces and the use of graduated colors.

But what we have here is, in effect, a last manifestation of the plastic type of painting. In Greece the seventh-century mosaics at St Demetrios (Salonica) and in Rome the seventh-century mosaics of Sant'Agnese, the eighth-century mosaics of the Oratory of John VII at the Vatican (judging by what is left of them), Santi Nereo ed Achilleo, and the early ninth-century mosaics at Santa Prassede, San Zeno, Santa Maria in Domnica and other churches, as well as certain frescos—all alike display tendencies quite other than, and indeed hostile to, classical tradition. Indeed this form of art tends, rather, to tapestry-like effects; the artist expresses his sensibility by means of juxtaposed touches of pure, glowing color and has recourse oftener than ever to the luminous effects of gold and imitations of pearls and gems. The jagged outlines circumscribing tracts of color make it plain that these artists felt no qualms about indulging in distortions of reality. Here the thoroughgoing re-interpretation of the legacy of ancient art as regards the human body (the process which began at Ravenna, following Dura) attains its apogee. To it we owe some remarkable achievements, such as the Virgin in the *Adoration of the Magi* (a mosaic dated to 705, originally in the Oratory of John VII at the Vatican, now in the sacristy of Santa Maria in Cosmedin) and the golden vault at San Zeno, with its procession of wraithlike saints limned in outline only, their ethereal bodies dissolved into the shining sea of the divine light.

Did Byzantine painting in the strict sense, that is to say the work produced in Constantinople, ever go quite so far as this in the direction of abstraction and geometric-chromatic expressionism—even in the time of the Iconoclasts? There is no knowing, but it seems quite probable, if we may judge by the one class of images of this period which has come down to us: the effigies of emperors on coins, which throughout the iconoclast age (727-843), but above all towards its close, under Theophilus, became exclusively geometric and linear.

The abandonment of this style is all the more suggestive since it synchronizes with the victory over Iconoclasm: a victory which not only ushered in a general revival of Byzantine painting but also brought back a conception of art more open to the influence of classical Antiquity. This, indeed, is the distinctive feature of Byzantine painting of the best period which now began, and which lasted until the end of the twelfth century. As compared with other Christian styles of the same period, the Byzantine way of handling a picture, notably the human form, and even landscape, always gives the impression of being nearer that of the Graeco-Roman past. If, however, we look into Byzantine works more closely, we not only find that this kinship had limits but, what is of even greater interest, that their artistic value is conditioned by the way these limits are defined. Obviously we may speak of a compromise between classical tradition and means of expression antagonistic to it, and thus stress the link between Byzantine art during the Middle Ages and that of the close of the classical era. But perhaps it is better to speak of an art language that, while using ancient words, adapts them to a more advanced syntax and takes into account the phonetic and semantic changes they have undergone in recent times. Thus the old words are given a new resonance and should be heard in a new way. Familiar to the philologist, this process has many analogies in the history of art, and the vicissitudes of mediaeval Byzantine aesthetic are particularly revealing in this respect. For we find in it, as at certain stages in the evolution of a language, two kinds of forms existing side by side: forms of the past which have undergone a gradual change in current use, and other forms of a purer style which have been brought into currency by more sophisticated artists.

The process of re-adjustment to classical prototypes seems to have begun for the most part in the illuminators' workshops, that is to say in co-operation with Byzantine men of letters who specialized in copying classical works and sometimes amending manuscripts made during the last phase of the classical era. These imitations of ancient illuminated manuscripts were remarkably successful, though admittedly they were no more than faithful reproductions of given prototypes whose style was thus embodied and perpetuated in the tenth- and eleventh-century copies. The climax of this classicizing art (so far as the miniature was concerned) was reached in the tenth century, and it was probably then that a parallel movement, in the art of non-religious carvings on ivory coffers, came to the fore. However, the antique style resuscitated in the ivories had nothing in common with the classicizing art of the contemporary miniature. In mural painting—the Byzantine major art—this reversion to a classical style did not make itself felt effectively until towards the second half of the eleventh century (at Daphni). Indeed one has the impression that under the Macedonian emperors (mid-ninth to mid-eleventh century) classical Antiquity did not play a basic part in the art of painting in general, but merely provided a repertory of models of various kinds that artists drew on as required; these borrowings go back to different periods and usually function within a well-defined range of works.

When in the ninth century the iconoclast ban on imaging was lifted, the painters' first reaction was to fling themselves wholeheartedly into the imitation of works anterior to the interregnum. But their enthusiasm tended to fritter itself away in representations of the plastic qualities of bodies and draperies; ungracious *revenants* from the Iron Age of the close of Antiquity, these dumpy, thickset figures with low foreheads and eyes set wide apart lacked both elegance and spirituality. To start with, only angels were immune from this earthbound, graceless presentation; however, before long they were joined by other subjects which the spiritualizing trend of mediaeval thought endowed with life, after its fashion. Thus from the close of the tenth century (in the miniatures of Paris MSS Grecs 64 and 70) we find two processes simultaneously at work; the infusion of an inner life into figures and a diversity of means of expression used for their portrayal —elongations, more varied renderings of forms and postures, the replacement of rigid frontal poses by asymmetry, and even a sporadic use of attitudes calling for fore-shortening. Following the miniatures, monumental painting in the eleventh century certainly benefited by the artists' study of ancient paintings and sculpture; indeed there are mosaics of this period (e.g. at Daphni) which look exactly like classical bas-reliefs with color superadded. But of prime importance was the fact that the study of ancient art, far from diverting the Byzantine painters from their constant objective—the intelligible—pointed the way towards it, and by a better route than in the past. For it is obvious that the miniatures of ca. 880 (Paris, MS Grec 510) and likewise the mosaics (ca. 850) in the Church of the Dormition at Nicaea are far from expressing the same intense religious emotion as the miniatures in the *Menologion* of Basil II (ca. 1000) and the Chios mosaics (eleventh century). The reason is that the Byzantine artist when imitating a classical motif invariably produced (however successful the imitation) a new version, charged with a new significance. Thus he made slight changes in the proportions of a figure and the different parts of a body; almost imperceptible deviations of the lines defining a face; harmonies and clashes of colors, and contour-lines integrating a figure into a unit of pictorial expression or, on the contrary, detaching it from that unit and giving it a separate aesthetic function.

As was the case with architecture at Byzantium in the Middle Ages, and in Italy during the Renaissance, the deliberate recourse to ancient forms did not divert painting from the otherworldly themes which were its chief concern, but aesthetically enriched it, by providing it with additional means of expressing them. Thus it would seem that the Byzantines of this period discovered what the Humanists were to discover later on: that the divine can be expressed most efficaciously by harmonies of line and color combined with flawless symmetry.

Byzantine painting of the best period (tenth to twelfth century) owes much to its preoccupation with balanced rhythm; this imparts to it a grave and noble (if a shade monotonous) quality, and a quasi-monumental aspect to even the smallest works. Indeed every miniature looks like the reduced copy of a fresco. Naturally enough these virtues found most scope in the decoration of buildings. In this field none could compete with the Byzantines in the Middle Ages, and the efficacy of their procedures can be seen at its splendid best. On the face of it, these procedures were simplicity itself, but the imperfect successes of their imitators show that this air of simplicity was deceptive.

The human figure was the unit by which the proportions of these decorations were determined. Thus the artist's first step was to decide on the size of the normative figure, as against that of the building to be decorated, and then to assign to all the figures dimensions proportioned to it. Also the human figure had to be adjusted (without the help of frames) to the architectural elements basic to the painted surface, and, being thus treated as integral to the architecture, was elongated or shortened, enlarged or incurved, as required.

In adapting the human body to an architectural *datum* the Byzantine artists showed quite amazing resourcefulness. For not only did the curved vaults and apses of the churches set them complicated technical problems, but classical tradition (and perhaps religious scruples, Man being "in God's image") forbade their straying too far from lifelikeness in depicting the human body, its proportions and attitudes. The difficulties the artists had to overcome are brought home to us when we see the mistakes made by rustic, imperfectly trained painters—in, for example, the frescos in churches hewn in the rock, in faraway Cappadocia. In fact many provincial frescoists never solved these problems satisfactorily; hence the frequent disproportion between figures near each other and the sometimes exaggerated size of heads or feet. As compared with pre-iconoclast art, tenth to twelfth century painting is remarkable for the lucidity of the composition, with its broad lines clearly indicated, and the large, judiciously proportioned empty spaces surrounding figures. The lay-out of mosaics and frescos, indeed of all mediaeval Byzantine figural art, is primarily determined by the interplay of lines and forms described above, and the same is true of the rhythms, proportions and balance of the composition.

But the over-all arrangement of Byzantine paintings, and indeed all Byzantine art, owes as much, if not more, to the artists' concern for color; indeed it is in this field that the originality of the Byzantines vis-à-vis classical tradition strikes us most. For though they innovated in their linework (notably when adjusting figures to decorative exigencies), it was above all with color that they achieved an expressive power unequaled in the painting of Antiquity. Their precursors in this field were obviously those earlier artists whose work in churches at Ravenna has already been discussed. During the Middle Ages there was a return, at Byzantium, to the rich effects of the early mosaics and the lavish use of gold, with warm tones of purple and deep, vibrant blues set off by passages of cool, limpid color and gold or sky-blue backgrounds.

As in the past, color was employed not with a view to imitating the natural hues of objects but to composing melodies or phrases which, in combination with a theme stated by the linework, interpreted it chromatically. Thus there were fixed color-schemes attached, like leitmotifs, to specific persons and enabling the spectator to know at once who was portrayed. To Christ pertained blue and cherry-red, sometimes picked out with gold; to the Virgin, all shades of blue; to St Peter, yellow and light blue; to St Paul, blue and claret-red; to Emmanuel-Logos, yellow streaked with gold. The conjunction of two or more figures, or of a hill with an edifice, gave rise to color harmonies, not uniform or obligatory, but drawn from a repertory of color combinations that had proved their worth, and it was by appealing to the sensibility of the eye to colors that the painter conveyed his message. While the range of colors is varied, the hues themselves are usually sober, more so than in the sixth century. Just as in the linear composition empty spaces emphasize the purity of the contours, so a white ground brings out the yellows, pinks and greens superimposed on it. In both cases we find the same limpidity, a like discretion—proof of a perfect balance between the painter's intentions and his means.

During the last phase of Byzantine art, however, this balance was upset, under conditions which have not yet been wholly elucidated. From the second half of the twelfth century on, and notably in the thirteenth and fourteenth centuries, Byzantine painters sought to treat the time-honored, traditional themes on more subjective lines. Moreover, the authorities who drew up their "programs" encouraged them to treat anecdotal or dramatic subjects such as the Childhood of Christ and the Passion, and in dealing with these subjects (which gave them more scope in this direction than the somewhat abstract themes of the past) painters could display more boldly their gifts of observation and their personal sensibility.

True, every first-rate Byzantine work of art bears the imprint of its maker—we need only compare a mosaic at Chios with one at Daphni to see this. But during the last centuries of the Empire works of art were far more individualized, both within the Byzantine area and in neighboring countries. Though artists now began to sign their works (e.g. at Nagoricino and Lesnovo in Serbia), nothing is known about them personally; all the same the decoration of each church is obviously due to a single master-craftsman, whose personality makes itself felt in the style of the painting and whose origin and training it might be possible to trace.

It is, to be sure, a matter of fine shades of difference; for at no time up to the fall of Byzantium do we find artists with personalities as strongly marked as those of the famous painters in Italy from the thirteenth century on. Nevertheless Byzantine painters made proof of much originality during this last period, notably in expressing their tragic sense of death and suffering or the fragile grace of childhood, and, secondly, in incorporating details of contemporary life in their renderings of biblical scenes. As early as the twelfth century these new tendencies were perceptible in the illustrations of the Sermons on the Virgin by the monk Jacobus of Kokkinobaphos and in the frescos at Nerezi (near Skoplje). Such indications of a new sensibility and a concern for imitating Nature became more frequent and persistent in thirteenth- and fourteenth-century frescos—at Milesevo, Sopocani, Mistra—and also in the mosaics of Kahrieh Djami and the Holy Apostles at Salonica. Thus an art whose commerce with physical reality had for many centuries been limited to reflections in it of the artist's personal talent now made a tentative move towards Nature. This approach to an imitative art was rendered easier by the existence of sequences of paintings, made in an earlier age, which depicted Gospel episodes and notably scenes of Christ's Childhood and Passion—precedents that were obviously discovered, and imitated, in the thirteenth and fourteenth centuries. For leanings towards realism were evident in those paintings in the ancient tradition, with their picturesque details, their evocations of hilly countrysides and architecture. Thus they provided at once a setting and an excellent starting-off point for Byzantine artists of the epoch of the Palaeologi, when they sought to record personal visual experience. Details taken straight from life and realistic or emotive fragments could easily be fitted into this framework, and this in fact was done. Thus once again, though in a different manner, Antiquity acted as the source of inspiration for a revival of Byzantine painting, and, since it was from paintings of this order that the art of Duccio and Giotto took its rise, the historical importance of these cycles of biblical paintings (linking up across the centuries with the miniatures in the Vienna *Genesis*) is considerable.

Yet, as is the case whenever ancient painting makes a direct contribution to Byzantine art, we find here too a latent incompatibility between them. Indeed, when all is said and done, it was Italian painting that benefited most by the renewed contacts of the Byzantines with paintings in the Hellenistic spirit. True, the mosaics and frescos mentioned above (and many others) justify the description of this style as the Byzantine Renaissance under the Palaeologi, for in many respects it was a revival of early Christian painting. What, indeed, could be more "antique" in appearance than some of the works at Sopocani and Kahrieh Djami, and what more "antique" in origin than the landscapes, decorative architecture and picturesque ensembles at Kahrieh Djami, and many of the Mistra paintings?

But the Byzantine artists capable of turning to good account the lessons in classical aesthetic furnished by Hellenistic models, were always a small minority. Indeed it would seem that in the first decades of the fourteenth century—the exact period when the Italians, by way of the Byzantines, were discovering in Hellenistic works so many pointers to new, epoch-making ventures in the realm of art—the Byzantines deliberately turned their back on ancient art and reverted to methods of a more recent past (which, for that matter, they had never quite discarded).

By this I mean that they did not follow up the lead given by their immediate predecessors and make Byzantine art an art of nature imitation as classical art had been and Quattrocento Italian art was to be. Similarly they no longer stressed their personal responses to simple human emotions as artists of the previous generation had done in their poignantly sensitive depictions of grief and childhood. Instead, they swerved away from the line of progress on which they had been advancing side by side with the Italians, sometimes even outstripping them, thanks to the superb technical tradition behind their work. Now, however, they reverted to conventional, time-honored methods of expression. Probably this reactionary movement stemmed from mistrust of all that went for "Latin." For emotional and imitative art had, soon after 1300, become characteristic of the West, and Orthodox painters may well have felt it incumbent on them not to approach art from the same angle as Italians and Franks.

Whatever the reason, there was a reversion to ancient methods, and to it we owe a host of paintings, new versions of old themes, in which the traditional qualities of Byzantine art are seen at their best. Once more we find that magnificent draftsmanship which transforms a person or an object into a "graphic phrase"—a phrase that flashes its message home to the beholder. Sometimes, indeed, the drawing is even more brilliant, more decorative than in the past; in fact some of the figures and scenes of action show that Byzantine art underwent a "baroque" phase in the fourteenth century. Bodies are elongated, attenuated, sway and writhe under elaborately built-up drapery; also in the drawing of the heads we find a new, experimental boldness, sometimes startlingly geometrical in conception. Color retains its old prestige, as the most potent means of expression and the backbone of the composition, but the range of colors now is wider than in the time of the Macedonians and the Comneni, when the aim of paintings, one might say, was to look like colored bas-reliefs. We find warmer, darker hues, more nuances and, as in the earliest period, juxtapositions of complementary colors. (Perhaps the Byzantine decorators retrieved this color magic by way of miniatures in the Hellenistic tradition.) As in the past, the painters of the age of the Palaeologi made no attempt to imitate the real colors of nature; for them, as it had always been for the Byzantine artist, the *sine qua non* was to create a picture valid in its own right, and to exploit all the possibilities of color—by its judicious distribution in patches at appropriate distances from each other, and by means of harmonies and clashes—so as, in conjunction with the drawing, to present to the beholder an artistic interpretation of a sacred theme and render palatable to him the formulas of an iconography hallowed by long tradition. Thus a gifted painter had ample scope for making good his personality— the high quality of so many works is proof of this—and, all the same, this conception of the artist's creative franchise was in strict conformity with the canons of the Church.

CRITICAL STUDY

ST DEMETRIOS. SEVENTH CENTURY (?). DETAIL. MOSAIC,
CHURCH OF ST DEMETRIOS, SALONICA.

FIFTH AND SIXTH CENTURY MOSAICS

There is much to be said for viewing the mosaics of Salonica and Ravenna in the course of the same journey; belonging to the same Early Christian period (fifth and sixth centuries), they have much in common, though each group has its distinctive characteristics. Indeed a comparative study of these mosaics would throw light on the local interpretations which those two great cities of the Early Byzantine era brought to the same art—one which, in point of fact, was essentially an art associated with cities, beginning with the great capitals in which imperial palaces set the fashion.

SALONICA

As remarked above, the mosaics at Salonica and Ravenna are akin, notably as regards their common denominator, by which I mean those more or less superficial aspects which belong to the period, and are frequent and widespread throughout it. I have in mind, for example, the wealth of ornamental compositions covering all the arches in the great basilica known as the Church of the Virgin styled "Acheiropoetos," and those in the small Oratory of Christ Latomos and in the niches of the circular Church of St George (all three fifth-century edifices). Most interesting of the mosaics are those in St George's, where they imitate Persian silks and carpets, with motifs of birds, palmettes and fringes. Lavish decoration was then in fashion and whole interiors were lined with mosaics, from the summits of domes and vaults to the pavements of buildings, both sacred and profane. The "rich" style seems to have touched its apogee in the fifth century; already in the next century, under Justinian, decorative artists began to reduce this plethora of ornamentation and enable the architectural structure to make its presence felt (see below, Sant'Apollinare Nuovo at Ravenna and St Sophia, Constantinople). Only Syria kept to the practice of sumptuous all-over adornment, as we learn from the decorations in the Ommiad palaces and mosques which in the seventh and eighth centuries carried on the methods of Syrian Byzantine art.

But the mosaics at Salonica and Ravenna are akin to each other also in their loftiest creations. The *Young Christ* in the apse of the Oratory of Christ Latomos at Salonica much resembles the majestic *Good Shepherd* in the Mausoleum of Galla Placidia at Ravenna. But at Salonica He is given the central place in a vision appearing to Ezekiel and another prophet, and this is why his face conveys not so much the imperiousness of Godhead as the eternal youth of Emmanuel the promised Son. The same freshness of inspiration is found in the likenesses of martyrs in the dome of St George's. However, we regretfully decided against including reproductions of either of these ensembles in the present work, despite their great aesthetic merits, since their true colors will emerge only after the cleaning now in progress. Meanwhile our plate of the *Good Shepherd* in the Mausoleum of Galla Placidia may perhaps do duty for the Christ Emmanuel in

ST DEMETRIOS AND DONORS. SEVENTH CENTURY (?). MOSAIC, CHURCH OF ST DEMETRIOS, SALONICA.

the Oratory of Christ Latomos, while in the mosaics of another church at Salonica, St Demetrios, we have portraits of martyrs which clearly derive from those at St George's, sometimes excelling, sometimes falling short of them.

This is a vast reliquary-church which, from the fifth century on, housed the relics of Demetrios the martyr, favorite saint of the Greeks. The mosaics we reproduce cannot be earlier than the sixth century and may well be seventh-century works. They are some of the many panels covering the walls of the Church of St Demetrios, whither hosts of pilgrims flocked to invoke the help of this miracle-working saint. Thus we have here *ex-votos* commemorating particular occasions and showing the saint attended by his protégés. Amongst them figure the two supreme authorities at Salonica—the Archbishop and the Governor—and, in several panels, children confided to the saint's protection. In all these panels the artists practiced a remarkable economy of means; thus the colors are sober almost to the point of meagerness, with cool tones predominating: whites and greys, green mingled with a little gold. We find the same austerity in the composition, built up with juxtaposed verticals, and likewise in the style. The space dimension is ignored; bodies have no volume and are replaced by curtain-like screens of drapery with straight-falling folds that purport to be the garments of the figures. But there is nothing abstract about the heads (shown in the characteristic frontal position) —that of Demetrios, for example, with its big, visionary eyes. All are wonderfully alive, and these portraits, though schematic, are full of personality. This is the same art as we shall see at San Vitale, Ravenna, in the groups including Justinian and Theodora, but here we have a less sophisticated, more spontaneous version, perhaps slightly later in date and more closely linked up with the cult of the icon.

The gradual stages by which the portrait progressed towards the icon are clearly brought out by a comparison of the portraits of St Demetrios in the church bearing his name and those of martyrs in St George's. Obviously the latter were placed too high to serve as icons; moreover, their extreme emphasis on the physical beauty of these heroes of the faith made them somewhat unsuitable for the veneration of the devout. When, in a later chapter, we deal with that special form of sacred art, the Byzantine icon, we shall revert to the St Demetrios mosaics, for they throw much light on the evolution and liturgical function of the images of Christ or saints which were treated as objects of worship. The votive mosaics at St Demetrios depict in one and the same panel the saint himself as he figured on his icons and also those who came to pray before them, as if they were contemporaries; this, materially speaking, impossible conjunction shows that these pictures were intended to convey the significance of religious contemplation in an easily understandable form.

VAULT DECORATION. FIRST HALF OF FIFTH CENTURY. MOSAIC, MAUSOLEUM OF GALLA PLACIDIA, RAVENNA.

THE GOOD SHEPHERD. FIRST HALF OF FIFTH CENTURY. MOSAIC,
MAUSOLEUM OF GALLA PLACIDIA, RAVENNA.

RAVENNA

Even more than Salonica, Ravenna is the locus classicus, so to speak, for fifth-
and sixth-century mosaic decorations; the only city in the world in which the earliest
tokens of its bygone glories are masterpieces of the art of the church mosaic. Capital of
the Western Empire in the fifth century, Ravenna was lavishly adorned with palaces and
churches during that period, and still more were built under Justinian when he made that
city the seat of the government of Italy, now incorporated in the one and only Christian
Empire. Throughout this epoch Ravenna was actually or potentially an imperial resi-
dence, if a relatively small one compared with the supreme seat of the imperial
government, Constantinople.

In this capacity Ravenna was the home of an aulic art and, more than in other
cities, the prestige of this art, sponsored by the Imperial Palace, made itself felt in the

local churches. And inevitably, like other minor residences of the Emperor, it came under the thrall of the metropolis, Constantinople, being chiefly influenced by the art of the Great Palace of Byzantium and its repercussions on church decoration. Not that the mosaics of Ravenna from the fifth to the seventh century must be regarded as a mere replica of those in Constantinople; by way of Milan and Rome the art of Ravenna linked up closely with Italian Christian art, many of its distinctive features being clearly traceable to an Italianate tradition. It is even possible that, when imported to Ravenna, the art of the imperial capital sometimes assumed forms that were unknown at Byzantium itself; for it was not in Constantinople but in Rome that the foundations of monarchical Christian art, and Christian art of monarchical inspiration, were laid (see Introduction). None the less at Ravenna more than elsewhere we are justified in suspecting, wherever the Ravennate mosaics seem inspired by the conceptions or ceremonial of the Court, that these are reflections of the art of Constantinople.

THE HOLY VIRGINS. AFTER 526. FRAGMENT. MOSAIC IN THE NAVE,
SANT'APOLLINARE NUOVO, RAVENNA.

The mosaics in the chapel which, though there is no certainty about this, is always called the Mausoleum of Galla Placidia, are at once the oldest at Ravenna and, aesthetically, the most stimulating, this being due to the smallness of the place in which they figure. Warm, vibrant colors flood the air and hold our eyes bewildered with their luminous profusion. Wherever we turn our gaze we see, strangely close at hand, a richly glowing tapestry, a starry night sky, a figure emerging from infinite depths of space, and we seem to feel the presence, immanent and intelligible, of the faith that calls to life and action, in a world of dreams come true: a martyr triumphant over the flames confronting him, white-robed apostles gazing in adoration at the cross, a shepherd tending his flock with the majesty of a King of Kings. The grandeur so convincingly imparted to the Good Shepherd and the saints by the mosaicists who worked in the Mausoleum is not only one of the major virtues of this decoration but also typifies one of the art forms which Byzantine art, from its origins in the city on the Bosporus,

THE HOLY MARTYRS. AFTER 526. FRAGMENT. MOSAIC IN THE NAVE,
SANT'APOLLINARE NUOVO. RAVENNA.

THE PALACE OF THEODORIC. BEFORE 526. MOSAIC IN THE NAVE, SANT'APOLLINARE NUOVO, RAVENNA.

handled with the most persistence and success, thanks to the pointers given by the triumphal art of the emperors. And this theme of the Roman "triumph," transposed into the Christian ambiance of the Other World, opens out vistas of infinity beyond the walls and vaults of the little Mausoleum at Ravenna.

CATHEDRAL
BAPTISTERY

The art of the mosaics in the Baptistery adjacent to Ravenna Cathedral—it is also known as the "Orthodox Church" and the "Baptistery of Neon"—is both similar and contemporaneous (I accept the traditional chronology). True, one is not, as in the Mausoleum, in almost direct contact with the mosaics; most of them are placed very high, in the apex of the dome, and can be seen only by bending back one's head. I am not greatly taken by one peculiarity of this decoration—its alternation of mosaics with stucco ornaments on a colored ground. All the same, the circular procession of apostles in the dome has a dazzling effulgence, a sumptuousness surely unique of its kind. In the Mausoleum the Shepherd was King, here the Galilean fishermen are princes; their white garments, studded with golden cubes, glitter like flakes of living light upon the vast blue expanse of the background. For this zone of the world supernal the color-scheme is white-blue-gold; on the lower register, vermilion reds and rather vivid greens are added to depict the world of Man redeemed, an Earthly Paradise, at once garden, fane and palace.

When, at Ravenna, we turn from the fifth-century mosaics to those of the sixth, we leave a world of white and gold on blue, and enter one of white, green and purple on gold; with star-strewn depths of darkness replaced by the all-pervading sheen of an ethereal golden light. Sumptuous ornamentation is relegated to secondary positions, or eliminated, while tall, stately figures are given pride of place in the big panels. In fact the human figure reigns supreme in the new order. Placed full-face, it is defined by level planes which, though they demarcate its boundaries in space, do not locate it in depth, as was done in the fifth century. Thus, from now on, the whole decoration lies flat upon the surface of the wall or vault which it adorns.

Can it be assumed that these changes reflect certain contemporary trends of the mosaic in Constantinople itself? The dating of the monuments is no guide, since the earliest set of sixth-century decorations at Sant'Apollinare Nuovo (prior to 526) was the work of the Ostrogoth king Theodoric, and thus anterior to the Byzantine reconquest by Justinian. On the other hand, in the choir of San Vitale, despite its famous portraits of that Emperor, the Empress and their Court, we find several motifs stemming from mosaics made at Ravenna in the previous century. Nor does the influence of Constantinople determine the choice of subjects: the only cycle of Gospel scenes in Sant'Apollinare Nuovo derives from the Latin liturgy (as pointed out by C. O. Nordström); the Apostles in the Baptistery of the Arians are modeled on those in the Cathedral Baptistery, and if any influence from the East is traceable in these sixth-century mosaics, it hails presumably from Palestine (e.g. the jeweled "Cross of Jerusalem" with a bust of Christ in Sant'Apollinare in Classe).

However I am convinced that by this time the art of the Byzantine capital had already made its influence felt in so many major works that it must have shaped the evolution of nearly all the local Mediterranean Schools, and thus the innovations we see here derived most probably, in the first instance, from Byzantium. Some general trends and also specific forms apparent in these sixth-century mosaics foreshadow later works of Byzantine art in the strict sense of the term: the bareness of the uniform gold background and the predominance given the human form; frontal poses of the figures; a special technique ensuring surface plasticity without creating an illusion of depth. To these we might add the emergence of a lengthy cycle of Gospel themes (e.g. in Sant' Apollinare Nuovo). For, after all, was not Byzantium, from the early Middle Ages on, the seat *par excellence* of churches adorned with religious images, and these in far greater numbers than anywhere in the Western world?

All the same, it is not absolutely certain that this practice was equally characteristic of Byzantium so early as the sixth century. True, some written accounts (and a group of frescos at Perustica in Thrace) indicate that it was not unknown to the Byzantines in Justinian's time. But it is no less significant that the great churches erected by that emperor in his capital were not embellished with iconographical decorations (see below, St Sophia). Here, too, Palestine may well have been the birthplace of a genre that Byzantium was to adopt enthusiastically after the Iconoclast interregnum.

To sum up, the sixth-century mosaics at Ravenna probably reflected the art of Constantinople as regards their innovations, but these innovations merely added some slight changes to an earlier art tradition that continued to hold its own.

THE SACRIFICE OF ISAAC. BEFORE 547. DETAIL. MOSAIC IN THE CHOIR, SAN VITALE, RAVENNA.

Here small rectangles filled with figures occupy the upper register of the side walls, and the Gospel scenes are crowded together. But the patches of color they form on the uniform gold ground necessarily extend right up to the edges of the rectangles, each of which serves to implement the over-all decorative pattern of the walls. Thus, given their distance, the first impression these scenes make on the spectator is that of compact blocks of strongly vibrant colors, amongst which the passages of "imperial color"—purplish violet—strike a resounding note. Next he will observe the serried masses of forms soberly rendered in straight lines or simple curves, with rhythmic

MOSES RECEIVING THE TABLES OF THE LAW. BEFORE 547. FRAGMENT. MOSAIC IN THE CHOIR, SAN VITALE, RAVENNA.

THE EMPRESS THEODORA AND HER RETINUE. FRAGMENT: DIGNITARIES OF THE BYZANTINE COURT. BEFORE 547. MOSAIC IN THE CHOIR, SAN VITALE, RAVENNA.

recurrences of certain graphic motifs or patches—symmetrical compositions, in fact, devoid of artifice or charm, or any quest of "glamour," and not so much lacking depth as spatial extension above the figures.

Undoubtedly there are reminiscences of ancient bas-reliefs behind these austere depictions and in this respect it is interesting to contrast them with the mosaics in the nave of Santa Maria Maggiore (Rome) which derive from cabinet-paintings, perhaps from miniatures. These sixth-century mosaicists benefited by the so to speak negative instruction of the procedures followed at Santa Maria Maggiore, for the tiny dimensions of the biblical characters there portrayed and the technique employed—that of the tinted sketch— obviously impaired the decorative value of these pictures. The Gospel scenes at Sant'Apollinare, on the other hand, are wonderfully effective as decorations and it is noteworthy that here the organization of space is entrusted solely to the human figure, all ornamentation being ruled out. The Byzantines kept to this method until the close of the Middle Ages. They were even to go farther when, suppressing the frame around an isolated figure, they placed it in direct contact with the architectural element it was called on to embellish.

In the Gospel scenes, level with the windows, large unnamed figures look down from glittering gold backgrounds. But most impressive in Sant'Apollinare Nuovo are the two processions of virgins and martyrs moving towards Christ and the Virgin. Of all extant decorations none other harmonizes so perfectly with the architectural lay-out of a basilica: two parallel rows of columns leading, bay by bay, up to the altar. Here architectural elements and mosaics march side by side, obeying the same rhythm, white columns of the virgins' and martyrs' bodies dividing up the wall-space. The emerald green of the soil brings out the brightness of garments and a golden sheen envelops the triumphal cortège. Christ and the Virgin have the majestic air of emperors with a body-guard of angels, and the vanquishers of death are about to lay down their crowns before them; nowhere else, indeed, has an imperial theme been remolded to such effect in a work of sacred art. Indeed there may have been a good reason for this, since it seems likely that in its original version—before Justinian had it modified—this mosaic contained portraits of Theodoric and his court dignitaries. If this be so, the depictions of the Palace of Ravenna and its seaport Classis would be appropriate enough; for, as the mosaic stands, there seems to be no good reason why the starting-point of a procession of saints hailing from many countries should be the palace and port of Ravenna—in a sort of far-fetched replica of the procession of sheep moving towards the Lamb of God from the two towns between which his ministry was accomplished: Bethlehem and Jerusalem. In the original version the persons leaving the palace and the port of Ravenna were perhaps Theodoric, his wife and his retinue, and the saints merely preceded them (in pursuance of an iconographical arrangement then in vogue) as their sponsors before Christ and the Holy Mother. Then the *damnatio memoriae* of the hated Arian king led, in Justinian's time, to alterations in the mosaic that changed its purport, though not its aesthetic effect—whose major qualities have likewise survived the misdirected zeal of subsequent restorers.

THE EMPEROR JUSTINIAN AND HIS RETINUE. BEFORE 547. MOSAIC IN THE CHOIR, SAN VITALE, RAVENNA.

CHURCH OF
SAN VITALE
It is on vaults that mosaics show to the best effect, doubtless because this form of art owes so much to the play of light on and within the tesserae, and curved surfaces, catching the light from innumerable angles, kindle a vast diversity of broken gleams and color harmonies. For, according to the angle of refraction, cubes of the same color may present a whole gamut of chromatic variations, and these are implemented by the changes of the light from one moment to another. In fact we have only to gaze at a mosaic for a while to see these changes taking place before our eyes, and imparting a curious pulsation, as if they were alive, to the decorations of the vault.

Fine as are the mosaics in Sant'Apollinare Nuovo, they are merely complementary to the architectural structure and do not, so to speak, replace it; pillars and ceiling are left undecorated and thus their functional values make a direct appeal to the beholder.

THE EMPRESS THEODORA AND HER RETINUE. BEFORE 547. MOSAIC IN THE CHOIR, SAN VITALE, RAVENNA.

But at San Vitale (consecrated in 547) the true depth of the choir is apprehended only in terms of the mosaic revetment clothing it from ground level to the summit of the dome, proliferating on to the arches between the pillars and across the full width of the lateral arches level with the galleries. The choir is, in fact, lined everywhere with mosaics that mask the solid structure of the walls so effectively as to suggest the presence of some penetrable substance, as in a carpet, behind the glowing film of color. Thus our gaze roves so easily and smoothly over flat surfaces and ridges, planes and curves, that it accepts this colorful vision of space created by the over-all polychrome revetment, on its own terms.

Once our gaze is thus acclimatized to the ensemble, it reverts to individual motifs, starting with the "tent of heaven" in which winged beings bear up the Lamb Triumphant

THE EMPRESS THEODORA AND HER RETINUE. DETAIL: THE EMPRESS THEODORA. BEFORE 547.
MOSAIC IN THE CHOIR, SAN VITALE, RAVENNA.

64

while, beneath Him, garlands of flowers and fruit of the four seasons conjure up the endless cycles of created Time, and the "tent" of the firmament is transformed into the semblance of a garden of paradise by the flora and fauna woven into its texture. Bright in the glittering livery of youth and preceded by winged figures proudly brandishing the monogram of the triumphant Redeemer, Christ sits in glory on the sphere of the Cosmos, welcoming into his celestial garden the saints and the donor of the church of San Vitale. The altar of this sanctuary of Christ is in the center of the choir and it is there that the rite of Salvation solemnizing his triumph over Death is ceaselessly reiterated. Prophets and events announcing Him before the Incarnation and, above all, offerings and sacred repasts prefiguring the Communion Service, are depicted on the

THE EMPRESS THEODORA AND HER RETINUE. DETAIL: HAND. BEFORE 547.
MOSAIC IN THE CHOIR, SAN VITALE, RAVENNA.

THE EMPEROR JUSTINIAN AND HIS RETINUE. DETAIL: THE EMPEROR JUSTINIAN. BEFORE 547.
MOSAIC IN THE CHOIR, SAN VITALE, RAVENNA.

THE EMPEROR JUSTINIAN AND HIS RETINUE. DETAIL: HEAD OF A COURT DIGNITARY. BEFORE 547.
MOSAIC IN THE CHOIR, SAN VITALE, RAVENNA.

side walls, to remind the worshippers at each service of its divine origin and symbolic meaning. Lastly there are some portraits of persons who participated, whether directly or indirectly, in the founding of this place of worship: apostles who founded the first churches, the martyrs who were objects of a special cult at Ravenna or San Vitale, and, finally, the emperor and empress who doubtless sponsored the building of this church. The two panels showing Justinian and Theodora with their retinues are world-famous, and rightly so; this is not only the earliest depiction in monumental art of a basileus and basilissa of the Eastern Empire, but by far the most impressive.

Indeed no other illustration of the Christian theocracy as embodied in Justinian, consecrated emperor of the Roman world, can vie with this. We see the Emperor and Theodora bringing their offering of bullion, with due pomp and ceremony, to a sanctuary of Christ, their heavenly Lord, in exactly the same manner as the saints and martyrs in Sant'Apollinare proffered their golden crowns to Christ and the Virgin. Perhaps the influence of the other mosaic explains the re-appearance here of the theme of the Magi (embroidered on Theodora's robe). The Byzantine monarchs were the "new Magi," that is to say princes on whom, *ex officio*, devolved the duty that the Kings of the East were bidden to perform on one memorable occasion at the dawn of the Age of Grace. It behoved them, too, to bring their gifts to the Church, and to perform ever and again an act of recognition of their Supreme Master and, by the same token, of their own status as his mandataries. Hence their place at the back of the choir, immediately below Christ the King; the divine Grace whose sanctity invests them magnifies their stature, makes their faces mask-like and inscrutable, imparts a stately rhythm to their attitudes—and even causes these to be repeated uniformly by the men and women of their retinue. Likewise it causes them to advance in silence, in a prescribed order; in the Palace, as in its art, only a ritual language of gestures unlike those of normal life could express the supramundane quality of the emperor. Sixth-century art had more than one device for wresting a vision of transcendence from the raw material of life, without masking the fact that the emperor and *a fortiori* the empress and her retinue were human beings. Thus the heads are frankly portraits, and the artist has spared no pains in rendering the garments faithfully down to the least detail. But, as against this he aligns and flattens bodies; indeed they seem emptied of weight and substance, floating in the void, without any real contact with the soil. These figures tread on air, can cross their feet without crushing each other's toes and, instead of looking where they are going, gaze straight at the spectator, or, rather, slew their heads round so as to reveal themselves full face. For despite their feigned impassivity, we feel they are conscious of being observed and of the parts they are enacting in the ceremony. This curious scene is sublimated by the magic power of art; by a profusion of colors, by glints of gold and pools of darkness, by flecks of vermilion, emerald green and white, by daring juxtapositions of exquisitely delicate hues (pearl-grey, dull purple, violet-tinged white) which, proliferating everywhere, transform the orderly array of figures into a carnival of color, a glittering haze of broken lights.

THE EMPRESS THEODORA AND HER RETINUE. DETAIL: PORTRAIT OF A PATRICIAN LADY. BEFORE 547.
MOSAIC IN THE CHOIR, SAN VITALE, RAVENNA.

THE EMPRESS THEODORA AND HER RETINUE. DETAIL: GROUP OF WOMEN.
BEFORE 547. MOSAIC IN THE CHOIR, SAN VITALE, RAVENNA.

VAULT DECORATION. BEFORE 547. FRAGMENT. MOSAIC IN THE CHOIR, SAN VITALE, RAVENNA.

The two portrait panels form independent pictures enclosed in decorative frames of an amazing sumptuousness. Also the artistic treatment of these "imperial images" puts them in a class apart, different from that of the large biblical compositions on nearby walls. Two of the latter we illustrate: the scene of Moses receiving the Tables of the Law on Sinai and that of Abraham entertaining the three angels in the plains of Mamre and sacrificing Isaac. Here the figurative art is more restrained; white forms clad in the stately garments of Antiquity stand out against a green background of grass and hills; but placed behind the angels and beside Moses are queer-shaped trees and plants and steep fantastic cliffs depicted in glowing, almost strident colors. Moreover, no observer can fail to be struck by the distinctively "impressionist" use of color evident in these landscapes.

THE EMPEROR JUSTINIAN AND HIS RETINUE. DETAIL: ARCHBISHOP MAXIMIAN. BEFORE 547.
MOSAIC IN THE CHOIR, SAN VITALE, RAVENNA.

Flooded with light, ribboned with handsome grey columns, this church is decorated with mosaics only in the apse and on a narrow stretch of wall preceding it. Thus there is no comparing this decorative scheme with that of San Vitale, though both churches were consecrated in the same year (547). The spacious apse gives us a distant view of a vividly green, sunny garden, rising in tiers, and centering it, the saint in prayer. A large cross within a circle is the leading theme of the composition, which also contains a curious *Transfiguration*, half descriptive, half symbolic, the symbolic portion (sheep= apostles) being a mere survival of a convention that had certainly lost all emotive appeal in the age of Justinian. Probably this hybrid imaging in the apse owed something to reminiscences of the Holy Land; certainly nothing in it seems to reflect the art of Constantinople. The two archangels guarding the entrance of the apse, on the other hand, bring us back to Byzantium and, by the same token, to the art of San Vitale. Clad like emperors and holding the *labarum* (sacred military standard), they have that regal dignity which the Byzantines so persistently associated with visions of the Christian revelation, expressing it in terms of the ceremonial of the imperial court. The subtle color orchestration, purple and gold predominating, is characteristic of this genre, and identical with that of San Vitale. Portraits (much restored) of Byzantine bishops and emperors round off the cycle at the foot of the apsidal vault.

WOMAN CARRYING A PITCHER. SECULAR ART. FIFTH CENTURY (?). MOSAIC PAVEMENT,
GREAT PALACE OF THE EMPERORS, CONSTANTINOPLE.

YOUTH AND DONKEY. SECULAR ART. FIFTH CENTURY (?). MOSAIC PAVEMENT,
GREAT PALACE OF THE EMPERORS, CONSTANTINOPLE.

CONSTANTINOPLE
THE MOSAIC PAVEMENT IN THE GREAT PALACE

Towards the close of Antiquity monumental painting was extended to pavements, and mosaics, even frescos (in suitably protected places), were used to decorate floors. These included, as well as every conceivable kind of ornament, figures and sometimes complete pictures. Obviously this practice catered to the taste for rich all-over decoration which, taking its rise in the third century, persisted until the Arab invasion. All the provinces of the Empire, from Britain to Syria (and even farther East, to the kingdom of the Sassanids), were affected by it, and Byzantium was no exception. There were mosaic pavements everywhere, in churches, in private houses and in the Baths of the Byzantine (pre-Iconoclast) period still to be seen in all parts of the Eastern Empire. Excavations at Antioch have revealed an enormous number of mosaics of this kind in the houses of wealthy residents, and these decorations testify to a very pronounced taste for figural art. From the aesthetic viewpoint, however, these mosaics are seldom of any great merit; in fact they almost always have the characteristic defects of mass-produced works.

Of much greater interest are the mosaic pavements recently brought to light in an imperial villa at Piazza Armerina in Sicily and in the Great Palace of the Emperors of the East in Constantinople. The former is dated to circa 300, and its style is obviously anterior to the flowering of Byzantine art. The other pavement, ascribed to the mid-fifth century and indisputably in the Byzantine spirit, is all the more precious to us since it certainly came from one of the leading workshops in the capital, and thus enables us to see the best that was being produced by way of the mosaic pavement under Theodosius II.

This mosaic adorns the floor of a portico in the Palace whose exact function has not yet been determined. Quantities of human figures, animals and plants, forming tiny independent scenes, are spread out on a uniform white ground. These are mostly hunting scenes, with an emphasis on "big game" hunting, but there are also charmingly idyllic glimpses of tranquil natural life and—as if to strike a contrast with these peaceful interludes—representations of fights between animals, or between animals and mythical monsters. The earlier mosaic, at Piazza Armerina, has points in common with that in Constantinople; these, however, are limited to the subjects, the style is very different. Starkly realistic at Piazza Armerina, it is more elegant, better balanced in Constantinople. Already it shows traces of the idealism which came to characterize Byzantine art for many centuries, and we even find certain type figures and faces that were to persist in the workshops of Constantinople over a long period. We reproduce two fragments of this mosaic; the one with the donkey is a sort of genre scene and illustrates the descriptive aspect of this art; the other shows one of those figures stemming from classical art which are so often found in mediaeval mosaics and frescos (cf. the picture of a woman at Nerezi, page 145).

MOSAICS AND FRESCOS IN ROME

The catastrophic decline of Italy's political power (from the end of the sixth century to the end of the eighth) coincided with the period when art of Byzantine provenance gained much ground in Rome. This was largely the work of Greeks and Levantines who, coming from South Italy or provinces of the Empire that had been overrun by the Saracens, and thereafter terrorized by the Iconoclasts, had made their homes in the ancient capital. The fact that no less than thirteen popes, between 606 and 741, were Greeks or Syrians shows how large an element of the Roman population was Byzantine, and this also accounts for the favor shown to Christian painting in the Hellenic style in the churches of Rome.

Mosaics of unmistakably Byzantine inspiration were installed in several papal foundations; for example the Oratory of San Venanzio, in the Lateran (built by John IV, 640-642), the Oratory of the Virgin in the Vatican (by John VII, 705-707), the Church of Santi Nereo ed Achilleo (by Leo III, 795-816). Here, without departing from Roman conventions, the artists employed by these popes included iconographical arrangements of a Byzantine order (the Virgin in the Orans position in the San Venanzio apse; a Transfiguration and two scenes with the Virgin facing the apse of Santi Nereo ed Achilleo; a whole cycle of Gospel scenes in the Eastern manner in the Vatican Chapel). Aesthetically, too, each of these works has certain features in common with contemporary Byzantine painting. Thus the eight martyrs in a row on either side of the apse of San Venanzio derive from a form of art that, in its turn, was derivative from the portraits of martyrs in the churches of St George and St Demetrios at Salonica. We shall find other works of this kind—but frescos, not mosaics—in Santa Maria Antiqua.

The mosaics at San Venanzio are still *in situ*, though much restored, whereas those in the Oratory of John VII were dispersed on the destruction of the old St Peter's of the Vatican and most of them are lost. One of the surviving fragments is the (incomplete) *Adoration of the Magi*, in Santa Maria in Cosmedin. Notable in this mosaic, which preceded by two decades the Byzantine emperors' campaign against "imaging," is the delicacy of taste and execution—the shy grace of the youthful Virgin holding forth the Child, and the angel rather bashfully presenting the Wise Men to her. The charm this fragment has for us, despite the restorations it has undergone, is largely due to the purity and softness of its hues, the quiet glow of its flat planes of color: blue interspersed with brown, a little red and green, many passages of white, and a uniform gold ground. Like the San Venanzio portraits of martyrs, this picture belongs to the type of Byzantine art exemplified in the mosaics in St Demetrios at Salonica. Of a later date than most of these, it stresses their tendencies towards "dematerialization"; space and even relief are ruled out, and no attempt is made to suggest plastic values. Noteworthy, too, is the artist's uncertainty as to the relative sizes of figures in a single scene; the disproportions are due not only to their respective ranks in the spiritual hierarchy but also to a disregard

ORATORY OF
POPE JOHN VII

POPE JOHN VII. 705-707. MOSAIC FRAGMENT FROM THE ORATORY OF POPE JOHN VII
IN THE VATICAN. GROTTE VATICANE, ROME.

THE ADORATION OF THE MAGI. 705-707. MOSAIC FROM THE ORATORY OF POPE JOHN VII
IN THE VATICAN. SANTA MARIA IN COSMEDIN, ROME.

of the classical injunction that man is "the measure of all things"—including the work of art. The over-all unity of the composition is ensured by solely formal means, a skillfully devised counterpoint of lines and patches.

In the Grotte Vaticane is another fragment from the Oratory of Pope John VII, showing the Pope himself with the square nimbus (of the living) behind his head and in his hands a model of his chapel. There is a curious imprecision in the calligraphy, as though the mosaicist's hand were trembling when he made the portrait of this Greek pope, with his long nose, big melancholy eyes and scarlet lips between a grey mustache and beard. Tracts of color are circumscribed by red and black lines of varying thicknesses, and everywhere the coloring is extremely subdued; indeed, were it not for these contour-lines, the pope's face (which has been restored) would almost merge into the gold background—all the more so since the latter is not quite uniform but variegated with small, colored tesserae.

ST ABBACYR. SEVENTH CENTURY (?). FRESCO, SANTA MARIA ANTIQUA, ROME.

From the seventh century to the ninth several popes commissioned mural paintings for this church which, though Roman, was largely patronized by Greeks and many of whose frescos were made by Greek artists. True, we have no warrant for ascribing to a Byzantine source the art of *all* the murals in this "diaconia" dedicated to the Virgin, which, like St Demetrios at Salonica, contained several votive pictures having no connection with each other. But of undoubtedly Byzantine origin and typically "Greek" are many of the icons reproduced on the walls and in niches at Santa Maria Antiqua. This holds good especially for a whole series of seventh- and eighth-century paintings still to be seen in the nave; the two here reproduced (quite independent of each other) were selected by us from a large number of greatly faded, often hardly visible frescos, as having kept something of their pristine brightness. These examples make us realize that but for this rapid deterioration (some fifty years have elapsed since the discovery of the basilica in the ruins of the Forum) Santa Maria Antiqua would have been a veritable museum of Byzantine painting—as in fact it was at the time when, in Byzantium itself, all such art was banned by the Iconoclasts.

CHURCH OF
SANTA MARIA
ANTIQUA

One of our plates, the *Archangel of the Annunciation*, while probably dating to the seventh century, recalls much older paintings and also the Castelseprio frescos. It differs from the latter by the heavy build of Gabriel's figure (e.g. the shoulder and neck) and the more careful, not to say labored modeling of the face. Moreover, following a practice typical of the close of Antiquity, the face, despite its very real beauty, is not illuminated by any intimation of an inner life—another difference between this art and that at Castelseprio.

The relics of St Abbacyr, an eastern physician-saint, were brought to Rome in the seventh century; the fresco we reproduce shows him enshrined in a niche and delving with his spatula in a medicine box. Like the mosaics in St Demetrios at Salonica, this seventh- or eighth-century fresco, with its over-lifesize head, is an icon transposed on to a wall. The graphic and expressive art of this hagiographical portrait is akin to that of the Coptic paintings at Bawit and Saqqara; indeed it is highly probable that they had a common source, since the headquarters of the cult of St Abbacyr, before it spread to Rome, was Alexandria.

THE ARCHANGEL OF THE ANNUNCIATION. SEVENTH CENTURY. FRESCO, SANTA MARIA ANTIQUA, ROME.

THE MURAL PAINTINGS AT CASTELSEPRIO

Situated in an isolated spot some twelve miles from Milan and even nearer Castiglione d'Olona (famed for its pictures by Masolino), a small church, hardly more than a chapel, was the scene in 1944 of the discovery of a group of early mediaeval frescos. Their style has no definite analogies with that of any extant mural decoration; which is why, in the absence of any written records, it has not as yet been possible to classify them. Thus a great many approximate dates, ranging from the seventh to the tenth century, have been suggested, and some have thought to see affinities between them and (1) such Roman murals as the frescos of Santa Maria Antiqua or the mosaics in the Oratory of Pope John VII, (2) Carolingian art, (3) Palestinian paintings prior to the Moslem conquest, and (4) works produced at Constantinople during the "Renaissance" under the Macedonian Emperors.

We might perhaps have excluded the Castelseprio frescos from the present work since their connection with Byzantine art is uncertain; indeed personally I think that they link up in not a few respects with the Western art of the close of the first millennium of our era. But, on reflexion, we decided to include the Castelseprio frescos in this Study of Byzantine Painting for the following reasons. So long as the problem of the Castelseprio frescos remains an open one, the omission of these world-famous paintings might well be deprecated; moreover, even assuming they owe nothing directly to Byzantium, they can tell us something anyhow about the sources that may have been drawn on by the Byzantine Masters; and, finally, so exceptional is the quality of the paintings in this small church in Lombardy that, whatever their provenance, they stand in a class of their own and—on the level of those lost masterpieces whose existence we can usually only guess at behind extant works—may probably be associated with one or other of the great schools of the early Middle Ages and particularly that of Byzantium.

All the paintings that have survived at Castelseprio figure in the tiny choir and chiefly in its apse, in which, above a painted socle, are two tiers of scenes depicting the Childhood of Christ, with large medallions inset at three points. The central medallion, facing the nave, contains a bust of Christ and is the only painting here that has the look of a mediaeval work. For all the others—i.e. the scenes depicting, as in Santa Maria Maggiore in Rome, the first part of the Gospel story, from the Annunciation to Mary and Joseph up to the Adoration of the Magi and the Purification—seem so reminiscent of pre-Christian classical art that at first glance one is inclined to regard them as directly stemming from the frescos of Campania or the Palatine. For, whether we study the heads or the draped bodies, their modeling, their freedom of movement, the sometimes intricate foreshortenings, or again the seated or recumbent figures, or those approaching or receding from the spectator, and the impression of real weight produced by them —everywhere we find that the painter has achieved the illusion of reality by employing the best classical procedures; and, what is even more striking, these effects seem to have cost him so little effort that one has an impression of spontaneous, almost unthinking

THE PURIFICATION. FRESCO, CHURCH OF CASTELSEPRIO.

THE ANNUNCIATION TO JOSEPH. FRESCO, CHURCH OF CASTELSEPRIO.

artistry. He copes no less successfully with the problems of rendering space, whether in landscape scenes showing hillsides dotted with ornamental buildings and cattle, or in architectural interiors.

The "antique" look of the Castelseprio paintings can be accounted for only if we assume they were made either at a very early date, say the fourth century, or else during a classical renaissance. But iconographical considerations preclude their dating to a period earlier than the sixth century and thus rule out the first alternative; nor is the second sufficient by itself to account for the origins of the art of Castelseprio, since from the sixth century on a very great number of schools of painting, in various places and at various times, attempted with more or less success to copy ancient models. Some have suggested that there may have been a very early—seventh century—renaissance, but certain details such as the cross on the halo of the Christchild are only paralleled in Carolingian works—and here perhaps we have a clue to the probable date of the Castelseprio frescos. Moreover, both the dynamism and the remarkable deftness of the "illusionist" drawing are characteristic of some Carolingian works (School of Rheims, notably the illustrations in the Utrecht Psalter). As against this, however, the facial types, the linear designs of folds and the feeling for plastic form, as well as certain decorative motifs such as the single pillar with a ribbon tied around it, have much in common with ninth- and tenth-century Byzantine copies of classical prototypes. True, the Byzantine miniatures, which are almost the only surviving illustrations of this kind of painting as practiced in Constantinople, are merely painstaking imitations of ancient originals, whereas the Castelseprio frescos reveal the happy ease of the *œuvre de maître*. But, for all we know, such Byzantine miniatures as have come down to us may well be craftsmen's reproductions of similar but far more brilliant pictures—pictures which recaptured as effectively as the Castelseprio frescos the spontaneity of the artists of the late classical age. In that case the originals copied by the ninth- and tenth-century Byzantine miniature-painters were much like the frescos in the little church in Lombardy, and it may well have been that similar models were used for Carolingian illustrations such as those in the Utrecht Psalter. Thus quite possibly we have in Castelseprio a vestige of an art which was the starting-off point for two simultaneous "renaissances," Carolingian and Byzantine, and also gave a lead to the Schools of Reichenau and Saint-Gall.

Whatever view be taken of this important historical problem, I feel convinced that the "antique" quality we find in the Castelseprio frescos is a distinctive mark, not of the crude and usually ponderous works of Late Antiquity, but of the achievements of one of the various mediaeval renaissances which tended to exalt—from the romantic angle—the elegance of truly classical models, while imparting to them the typical imprint of mediaeval spirituality.

The Castelseprio frescos are the work of a very great artist and this fact lessens our chances of assigning him a place in the main stream of the art of his time. Thus, whether he was actually Byzantine, or only indirectly associated with Byzantium (or even quite independent of it), we should be chary of attempting to trace the art he stands for—when we seek to "place" it historically—to any specific art current, whether Italic or Constantinopolitan, of his day; in fact we should do better to picture him as initiating that current. A masterwork in the "antique" manner, these Castelseprio frescos constitute a milestone in the history of early mediaeval "renaissances."

MOSAICS OF THE MIDDLE AGES

So long as there was a Byzantine Empire mosaics of all kinds remained in favor, and especially mosaic decoration of the walls and vaults of palaces and churches; for the good reason that, since experience had shown that no other kind of decoration was capable of producing such gorgeous effects, it was deemed worthiest to adorn the House of God and the imperial residences.

We have already spoken of its earliest manifestations, in fifth-, sixth- and seventh-century churches. As a matter of fact during this period mosaic decoration flourished everywhere, from Gaul to Persia. Subsequently, however, it was much less widely employed, indeed Byzantium alone remained wholly faithful to it. This explains why there are so few mediaeval wall mosaics that are not either Byzantine or imitations of Byzantine works.

It seems unlikely that at any time the decoration of churches and palaces with mosaic pictures altogether ceased at Byzantium, though not a single work produced during the iconoclast interregnum (727-843)—anyhow in the countries then under the domination of the heretic emperors—has survived. The reason is not that the Iconoclasts put a wholesale ban on church decoration, but that all the works produced during that period (notably murals in churches combining hunting and circus scenes with ornamental compositions) were destroyed, once iconographic decorations and the cult of icons became once again the order of the day. Thus for a period of approximately two centuries we have not one Byzantine mosaic of any importance, and actually, since not a single ensemble of Byzantine mosaics belonging to the period between the sixth and eleventh centuries has survived, the gap is still wider, extending over no less than five centuries.

Under these circumstances it is not surprising that when it makes its reappearance during the Middle Ages, the art of the Byzantine mosaic presents many differences from what it had been during the fifth and sixth centuries. True, there is no question as to the continuity of this art—which indeed is unmistakable. Nevertheless the changes, understandable enough when we take into account the long period of time that had elapsed, are no less apparent, and for this reason it is convenient to deal with mediaeval mosaics in a separate chapter. On the other hand, our lack of material for so many centuries rules out any possibility of tracing the development, stage by stage, of the art whose flowering is to be seen in the mediaeval mosaics and which, in the tenth and eleventh centuries, gives the impression of being completely stabilized, though by no means stereotyped. For obviously the Byzantine mosaics belonging to this period were not produced by the same or even similar groups of craftsmen; indeed they reflect traditions of quite different schools. But, given the lack of surviving monuments, there is no means of tracing the origins or evolution of these schools.

Thus we shall deal with the various types of mediaeval mosaic one by one and in their chronological order, without, however, wishing to suggest that the forms of art

THE VIRGIN, PROTECTRESS OF CONSTANTINOPLE. DETAIL: THE CHILD JESUS. ST SOPHIA, CONSTANTINOPLE.

we find in the earlier mosaics necessarily led up to those of later ones. However, before discussing works of the tenth, eleventh, twelfth and fourteenth centuries, we shall begin with a rapid survey of the mosaics in St Sophia, for these panels are not merely master-pieces in their own right but, having been made at different dates, give us some idea of the Constantinopolitan prototypes of the works which have survived in other regions of the Empire. In fact, viewed as a whole, from both the technical and the aesthetic standpoint, the St Sophia mosaics provide as it were a cross-section of the art of the Byzantine mosaic during several centuries.

As regards the other mediaeval mosaics dealt with in the course of this work, we have thought it best to keep to a small selection of outstanding and significant works and to study them in some detail, rather than to give a hasty panoramic view of the general scene. Our first choice has fallen on two complete eleventh-century church decorations, one on the island of Chios, the other at Daphni near Eleusis (in the neigh-borhood of Athens), and also on the decoration of the narthex of an early fourteenth-century monastery church at Constantinople, usually known under its Turkish name of Kahrieh Djami. Naturally we are well aware that other excellent mosaics can be seen in Greece, in Constantinople and elsewhere, and that each has notable aesthetic qualities peculiar to itself. But the examples named above and illustrated here will suffice to give a good idea of the more vital aspects of Byzantine mosaic art in the Middle Ages.

During this period Byzantine church decorations, whether in painting or mosaic, had two invariable characteristics; they were practically always iconographical (no other school of Christian painting ever employed religious subjects so copiously and persistently), and every detail is regulated by an iconographical program, rigorously laid down and formulated. Since this program allowed so little latitude, all church decorations of the eleventh and twelfth centuries were much alike, all the more so because the architectural lay-out of the churches also conformed to a standard type. The structure was invariably cubical, crowned with a central dome (sometimes with other domes as well), and was intended to present a symbolic representation of the Christian cosmos. The function of the figures portrayed was to make known the dwellers in this cosmos, each being given his appointed place: God Almighty (Pantocrator) in the dome; the Virgin in the choir; the saints at a lower level, on arches, vaults and walls. And since the Kingdom of God came to include the earth and mankind only after the Incarnation—mystically reiterated in every Mass solemnized by man in any church whatsoever, and mirroring the adoration of God by the angelic hosts—the story of the Incarnation, that is to say a cycle of Gospel scenes, was added, from the tenth century on, to the painter's program. This iconographical arrangement was followed in the churches of Chios and Daphni (illustrated here) and in the churches of St Sophia at Ochrid and at Nerezi, whose frescos we shall deal with later.

There was comparatively little deviation from this program until the thirteenth and fourteenth centuries when, though the general scheme of church decoration was not radically altered, we find a tendency to increase the number of scenes with figures, and to depict more saints and incidents from Holy Writ and the lives of the saints.

Apocryphal episodes of Christ's childhood and detailed renderings of the Passion now were often given a large place on the walls. Our illustrations of the ultimate phase of Byzantine art are drawn from decorations of this kind: the mosaics at Kahrieh Djami in Constantinople, and mural paintings (more typical than the mosaics of the art prevailing in this period) in some thirteenth-century churches (Milesevo, Sopocani), and also fourteenth-century paintings (in the Aphentico, the Peribleptos and the Pantanassa at Mistra, and at Gracanica in Macedonia).

Foundations of the Serbian kings, Milesevo and Sopocani are both in Serbia. The frescos in these churches certainly owe much to local artists, but it is none the less evident that these artists were inspired by authentically Byzantine originals that no longer exist. Thus these Serbian frescos have much documentary value for the light they throw on Byzantine painting in the large during the thirteenth century.

CHRIST-HOLY-WISDOM. END OF NINTH CENTURY. MOSAIC IN THE NARTHEX, ST SOPHIA, CONSTANTINOPLE.

CONSTANTINOPLE: ST SOPHIA

St Sophia was not only the "Great Church" of the Byzantines, the cathedral-church of Constantinople, but, above all, the chief sacred edifice of the Christian Empire, whither its earthly sovereign, the Basileus, resorted to worship Christ, its heavenly ruler. Founded by Constantine, several times renovated, and wholly reconstructed by Justinian between 537 and 562, St Sophia has almost miraculously escaped the ravages of man and time, its sixth-century architecture and a large part of the interior decoration being still intact. The vertical wall surfaces were faced with slabs of polychrome marble, while arches and vaults up to the summit of the gigantic dome were adorned with mosaics. Older than Byzantium, this lay-out was always followed there whenever mosaics were employed for the decoration of sacred edifices.

Dozens of panels in mosaic, many of which certainly go back to Justinian's reign, can still be seen in this vast edifice. So numerous are they that there is justification for the view that from the foundation of St Sophia in the sixth century until the ninth, its decoration—apart from ornaments—consisted solely of crosses on a gold ground and, at the base of the great dome (these, however, may be ninth-century additions), four golden cherubim. Thus while conspicuous as to its size, this decorative scheme was above all remarkable, aesthetically speaking, for its extreme simplicity. To the fine proportions of the crosses standing out from a uniform ground and still more to the splendor of that vast, glittering expanse of gold is due the wonderful aesthetic effect of this noble achievement of the Justinian epoch, which was contemporary with the more iconographically treated and elaborate decorations at Ravenna.

But though, at the time of its foundation, no place was given in St Sophia to picture sequences adapted to its structure and befitting its unique liturgical function in the Byzantine world, a number of mosaics dealing with religious and historical themes were added subsequently, at various dates. The nave and choir under the great dome were decorated in the ninth and tenth centuries, according to a set plan, which will be

CHRIST-HOLY-WISDOM. DETAIL: LEO VI RECEIVING THE INVESTITURE OF HOLY WISDOM. END OF NINTH CENTURY. MOSAIC IN THE NARTHEX, ST SOPHIA, CONSTANTINOPLE.

described later. All the other mosaics in St Sophia, however, are quite independent of each other; they do not fit into any coherent decorative pattern, nor, as regards their subjects, are they concerned with the demonstration of general religious ideas. For, in fact, they are *ex-votos*, in other words offerings made in pursuance of a vow, in recognition of divine or saintly favors bestowed on individuals, and usually (it would seem) *ex-votos* set up by Emperors who, to our regret, had not the habit of adding inscriptions to explain what particular incidents they were intended to commemorate. All the imperial *ex-votos* which recent cleanings have brought to light beneath the overlay of Turkish whitewash are located in peripheral areas of the Great Church—in the narthex, south lateral vestibule, south gallery. I question if the relegation of these *ex-votos* (accompanied by the portraits of the imperial donors) to the outer portions of the edifice should be set down to Christian humility; in several other churches at Constantinople, for example in the Church of the Palace of Blachernae, the emperors did not hesitate about installing their portraits in the choir itself.

But the Byzantines had always a very lively sense of the correlation between the mural picture and the part of the edifice in which it was placed; its scale and proportions being determined by the architectural setting. Thus the almost overpowering size of St Sophia ruled out to all intents and purposes the presence of any portraits of individuals in the nave, and the votive pictures were installed in the periphery, where the height was less and there was an abundance of wall surfaces of suitable dimensions available; or else in lunettes which provided appropriate architectural settings for them. Thus the *ex-votos* in the galleries occupy well-defined wall spaces on which a whole composition fell naturally and harmoniously into place; while in narthex and vestibule the same function was assigned to semi-circular niches over doors.

No records or inscriptions give us any clue as to the date or dates of the various mosaics in the nave, that is to say the figures of prophets and canonized bishops on the large side walls of the church, below the dome. However, a fragment of an inscription still exists *in situ*, giving us to understand that the mosaics in the apse were made immediately after the victory over Iconoclasm, that is to say in 843. Leaving aside for the moment the problem of the dates of the mosaics which recent cleaning operations (under the supervision of the late Thomas Whittemore) have brought to light in the nave and choir of St Sophia, we will begin by noting their themes and the positions assigned them in relation to the structural lay-out of the edifice. Culminating in the Christ Pantocrator at the summit of the dome these mosaics formed a coherent whole closely akin to the iconographic ensembles that, according to contemporary accounts, adorned some churches built and decorated at the close of the ninth and the beginning of the tenth century (foundations of the emperors Basil I and Leo VI and their contemporaries). In the St Sophia mosaics we have one of the oldest versions of an iconographical arrangement that subsequently become customary: Christ in the dome, the Virgin in the apse, and prophets and saints, surrounding Christ, on the walls of the nave. We have already, in dealing with eleventh-century mosaics that maintained certain essential characteristics of this decorative lay-out, described the symbolism behind it.

Opinions differ amongst archaeologists as regards the dates of the mosaics that have escaped destruction, especially those in the choir: The Virgin and Child Enthroned and the angels preceding her on the arch facing the apse (only one of these angels has survived). Personally I incline for the ninth century, basing this dating chiefly on the obvious stylistic kinship of these works with the Nicaea mosaics (choir of the Church of the Dormition). Thus the mosaics in the St Sophia choir are presumably the originals referred to in the inscription accompanying them though they evidently underwent some restoration at a later date.

It is well known that the incorporation of holy images in the decoration of St Sophia (on the initiative of Photius) was a slow and gradual process; indeed the very hugeness of the edifice told against rapid work. As regards the dating a noteworthy point is that, amongst the colossal effigies of canonized bishops placed high up between the windows of the side walls under the dome, we find Ignatius, patriarch of Constantinople (who reigned until 877) depicted as a saint. However speedily he may have been placed in the canon of saints, this mosaic and the group of pictures around it can hardly be dated earlier than the first half of the tenth century.

This brings us to the period of the finest Byzantine achievements in pictorial art, and assuredly the "bishops" and "prophets" at St Sophia will rank among the world's masterpieces, once they are better known. For the coat of plaster covering them was stripped only quite recently and, pending the publication of a fully documented and illustrated account of these noble works, they are known only to a privileged few. With their rigidly frontal poses, broad shoulders and thick-set bodies, these figures, as seen from the center of the church, seem hardly more than motifs placed there to animate or lend an air of lightness to the walls of the nave beneath the dome (without, however, impairing their architectonic values). But as we draw nearer, these stately figures, which at a distance seem mere isomorphic elements of a decorative pattern, become individualized; every head conveys the impression of a strongly marked personality and we feel that each of these men "habituated to high thinking" (as Stendhal said of the saints in the St Mark's mosaics) had his private vision of the Christian verities and was fully conscious of a personal vocation allotted him by God.

We have, for example, the portrait, imbued with serene majesty, of that most famous archbishop of Constantinople, St John Chrysostom, and it is interesting to compare this portrait with another likeness of the same saint made two centuries later, in the Palatine Chapel, Palermo (see page 129). The differences between these two hagiographical portraits illustrate the remarkable progress of the ascetic ideal amongst the Byzantines in the interval.

Characteristic of all these paintings is the seeming simplicity of the execution, combined with highly adroit craftsmanship. Notable above all is the extension to mosaic of the procedures of painting with the brush (gradation of tones, close attention paid to relative dimensions and to the placing of cubes of various colors). But however far the mosaicist goes in the way of imitating painting, his tact and training prevent him from overstepping the limits beyond which his work would lose some of the special virtues of

THE VIRGIN, PROTECTRESS OF CONSTANTINOPLE. DETAIL: THE EMPEROR CONSTANTINE THE GREAT.
MOSAIC IN SOUTH VESTIBULE, ST SOPHIA, CONSTANTINOPLE.

ST JOHN CHRYSOSTOM. TENTH CENTURY. MOSAIC IN THE NAVE,
ST SOPHIA, CONSTANTINOPLE.

mosaic: a singular vibrancy of color due to the obligatory juxtaposition of tesserae of different hues, and the refraction of light at different angles caused by the necessarily distinct position of each cube—the result being that particular luminosity which is basic to the art of the mosaic.

On the threshold of the nave we are confronted by a mosaic in the narthex. It stands above the main entrance, known as "the imperial door," and depicts an emperor kneeling before Christ Enthroned and confronting two symmetrical medallions, one of a woman draped in a mantle, the other of an angel. The location of this mosaic stresses its importance; for it was customary to portray the patron saint of a church above the entrance. Now, since the "Great Church" of Constantinople was dedicated to St Sophia, in other words to Christ as the embodiment of Holy Wisdom, one would expect *a priori* that the mosaic over the main entrance would illustrate this theme. This hypothesis is, moreover, confirmed with reasonable certainty by a detailed study of this mosaic, in the light of certain sapiential texts and the glosses on them (as will be shown in a work that Miss M. T. d'Alverny will shortly publish on the Iconography of the Holy Wisdom).

The presence of an emperor at the feet of Christ-Holy-Wisdom adds a further confirmation of this view. The Basileus in question, as has long been known, is Leo VI (886-912). In the sermons of this philosopher-emperor, and particularly in his homily on the Annunciation, we find all that is needed to elucidate this mosaic on the lines described above and also his reasons for choosing this particular grouping (Christ Enthroned, attended by two personages figuring in the Annunciation, the Virgin and the Archangel Gabriel). Thus above the entrance of the greatest church in the Empire the Basileus depicted his heavenly ruler, Christ-Holy-Wisdom, with himself kneeling at his Master's feet receiving the investiture of Wisdom. In short, this mosaic defines and celebrates in terms of art the supreme power in the Byzantine Empire, governed by Christ through his vicegerent on earth, the Emperor.

With its robust, somewhat ponderous composition this mosaic is a distinctively ninth-century work. The throne is low and bulky; Christ's figure is thick-set, the hands and feet disproportionately large as compared with the head, while the highly expressive face is broad and flat. All faces have strongly marked features: big broad noses, large eyes. Modeling is indicated by tracts of almost uniform grey-green shading, with white or pale-pink highlights on the bodies. Contour-lines are clearly marked, even within the masses of hair and beards. So far as garments are concerned the color-scheme is sober, with white, grey-green and gold predominating; thus the general effect is that of a delicately tinted low relief, set off here and there with gilding. There is no denying that this is a rather clumsy work—a fact which, in view of the importance of the place assigned it, goes to show that at this time there were no more competent mosaic-makers available; probably because, since the downfall of Iconoclasm, there had so far been relatively few opportunities for practicing this art.

If, instead of entering St Sophia through the atrium, we employ the south entrance, we find in a vestibule of the narthex, above the door, another mosaic which likewise recalls a fact of much importance as regards the religious life of the Byzantine Empire: the fact that Constantinople was placed under the special protection of the Virgin. This mosaic, too, was made as an independent unit and thus may be assimilated to the imperial *ex-votos*; all the more so since it contains portraits of emperors. But here the portraits are retrospective and no name of a Byzantine basileus is appended to this work, which

CHRIST ENTHRONED BETWEEN THE EMPEROR CONSTANTINE IX MONOMACHUS AND THE EMPRESS ZOË.
ELEVENTH CENTURY. MOSAIC IN SOUTH GALLERY, ST SOPHIA, CONSTANTINOPLE.

has an iconographical kinship with the images graven on the seals of the priests of
St Sophia. Perhaps commissioned by a patriarch of Constantinople, this mosaic, judging
by the style, may be assigned to the beginning of the eleventh century, possibly to the
end of the tenth.

While, in pursuance of the monarchical tradition of Byzantium, every sovereign
ranked *de jure* as a deputy of Christ, who, under a personal delegation of authority,
owed his investiture to his heavenly monarch, the Church, on the other hand, claimed
as peculiarly her own—on posthumous grounds—two Byzantine emperors, Constantine I
and Justinian I. The former was officially canonized, the latter assimilated to the saints,

THE VIRGIN AND CHILD BETWEEN THE EMPEROR JOHN II COMNENUS AND THE EMPRESS IRENE.
TWELFTH CENTURY. MOSAIC IN SOUTH GALLERY, ST SOPHIA, CONSTANTINOPLE.

and both were honored by commemorative services in churches. The St Sophia mosaic illustrates what the Church regarded as the most meritorious acts performed by these two monarchs: Constantine's dedication of the city he had founded to the Virgin, and Justinian's presentation of St Sophia, whose final form was his creation, to the Church.

Historically, the juxtaposition of the two emperors in one scene is a glaring anachronism; more important is the light thrown by this mosaic on the way the Church turned to account the legends and iconography associated with them, the incidents in their respective careers which here are glorified being the donation to the Mother of God of the city of Constantinople and that of its Great Church. Thus, while the mosaic in the narthex gives us the imperial view of the relations between Church and State, that in the vestibule gives its ecclesiastical version. The former shows an emperor reigning by grace of the Holy Wisdom; the latter extols the virtue of monarchs who fulfill their duties as Christian princes by presenting their foundations, cities and sacred edifices to the Holy Virgin.

The art of this mosaic is more coloristic, as we can see when we examine the small figure of the Infant Jesus snugly ensconced on His mother's knees and the garment worn by her, which acts as a backcloth to the figure of the Child. The blue of Mary's cloak is composed of a tesselation of numerous shades of blue and there is an amazing wealth of colors in the tiny cubes composing the Child's head, features, blue eyes, full cheeks, neck and hair. We find the same feeling for color in the rendering of Christ's tunic, with red-brown folds spanning the cloth of gold and soft white highlights misting the luster of the metal. The supple grace of the Mother's hands makes an effective contrast to the plumpness and robustness of the Child's.

The symmetrical depictions of Constantine and Justinian are not portraits but hagiographical representations; hence their extreme—if doubtless factually unwarranted—similarity, which the painters have not attempted to mitigate in any way. The strong feeling for color, characteristic of the whole panel, is particularly evident in the portrait of Constantine which we reproduce. Admirable indeed is the skill with which the tesserae of glass and stone, of so many diverse hues and carefully selected sizes, are handled by the mosaicist. In the modeling of the face, however, the monastic ideal which then was gaining ground at Byzantium, has prompted the artist to stress the wrinkles and the gauntness of the emperors' cheeks, and by the use of greenish shadows he gives an ascetic cast to their faces. The obvious effort made to bring out the plastic volumes of each face points to the vogue of classical art at Byzantium during the tenth century.

The galleries in St Sophia formed series of large, deep recesses from which it was possible to watch the services taking place in the choir, without being seen by the crowd of worshippers in the nave. In fact they served as gynecaea, the south gallery being reserved for the use of the Emperor's family, who performed their devotions there secluded from the public eye. Thus it is natural enough that we should find on the walls of this gallery—the "Royal Box" as it were—two votive mosaics commemorating the ceremonial offerings made by the rulers to St Sophia.

These two mosaics, which are situated on the east wall of the gallery, in the part of it nearest the chancel, are independent units and there was an interval of over fifty years between the dates when they were made (mid-eleventh and early twelfth century). Stylistically, too, they differ, though their iconographical scheme is practically identical: an emperor and empress (accompanied in one case by their son) on either side of Christ or the Virgin, to whom they are presenting a purse of silver and a roll of parchment (i.e. donations). The making of offerings of this kind to the "Great Church" was a customary, indeed a ritual gesture, and hence obligatory on the sovereigns. And the iconographical arrangement of these pictures, being no less "standardized" than the rite itself, allowed no scope to creative originality on the artist's part. It always took the form of a tripartite,

THE VIRGIN AND CHILD BETWEEN THE EMPEROR JOHN II COMNENUS AND THE EMPRESS IRENE.
FRAGMENT: THE EMPRESS IRENE. TWELFTH CENTURY. MOSAIC IN SOUTH GALLERY, ST SOPHIA, CONSTANTINOPLE.

carefully balanced composition, with a sacred personage, usually taller than the others or placed on a slightly higher level, forming the axis of an equilateral triangle and the apex of a pyramidal lay-out. There are uniform gold backgrounds in both panels, with the names and titles of the emperors inscribed in dark lettering on the gold ground.

Historically, the earlier of these mosaics has the greater interest, in view of the alterations that can be detected in it. The persons shown are Constantine IX (Mono-machus) and his wife Zoë on either side of Christ Enthroned. They reigned from 1042 to 1050, but only the heads of the three figures and the parts of the inscriptions bearing Constantine's name can be assigned to their reign; it is clear that they were substituted for other heads and a former emperor's name. The explanation is simple: Zoë was that remarkable woman who was successively married to three basileis: Romanus III, Michael IV and Constantine IX, and this mosaic originally showed her as the wife of one of Constantine's predecessors. On her third marriage the picture, now being ana-chronistic, was brought up to date. It is even possible that there had been a previous rectification when Zoë married Michael. From the viewpoint of the art historian one aspect of these alterations is of much interest for the light it throws on the remarkable aesthetic sensibility of the Byzantines; and this is that all three heads—not only those of the emperor and empress, but Christ's as well—were remade. For while there is just the possibility that Zoë's portrait was expunged at the same time as that of her second husband, by their common enemy Michael V (Calaphates) during his brief reign, never would any Byzantine emperor have dared without some very good reason to tamper with a head of Christ. It was not because they had been damaged that the heads of Zoë and Christ were remade at the same time as the Emperor's, but for purely aesthetic reasons; because the juxtaposition within a single panel of incongruous pictorial elements would have offended Byzantine taste.

In this panel—as also in some eleventh-century miniatures produced by the Court workshops—we can see the great importance the Byzantines now attached to draftsman-ship. Christ's head and the uplifted hand are revealing in this respect, as is the treatment of the drapery. If rather stiff, Christ's garment is finely executed, and its elaborate, carefully thought out design serves chiefly to build up an expressive patch of blue in the midst of the gold field of the mosaic. Characteristic of all the "official" portraits of emperors is the meticulous attention, reminiscent of jewelers' work, given by artists to costumes and insignia; studded with pearls and precious stones and patches of enamel, they encase figures like sumptuous coats of mail. Under this carapace, composed of severely linear patterns, bodies seem flat or almost so, no effort being made to bring out their plastic qualities. Only the head emerges, and only the pink face, between the necklet and the crown, gives the impression of three-dimensional volume, though even here plastic values are very discreetly handled and, except in the bulging cheeks, line-work is given the leading role. Notable, too, is the curious tendency to widen faces, giving them a faintly Mongolian air. This was probably a passing vogue and perhaps stemmed from Armenia, which was occupied by the Byzantines and garrisoned by imperial troops during the first half of the century.

ALEXIOS. TWELFTH CENTURY. DETAIL. MOSAIC IN SOUTH GALLERY, ST SOPHIA, CONSTANTINOPLE.

THE "DEESIS." FRAGMENT: THE VIRGIN MARY. END OF TWELFTH CENTURY. MOSAIC IN SOUTH GALLERY,
ST SOPHIA, CONSTANTINOPLE.

THE "DEESIS." FRAGMENT: ST JOHN THE BAPTIST. END OF TWELFTH CENTURY. MOSAIC IN SOUTH GALLERY, ST SOPHIA, CONSTANTINOPLE.

Our second panel may almost certainly be dated to 1118, the year of the coronation of John II (Comnenus) and his wife Irene, daughter of a saint, King Ladislaus of Hungary, and herself a saint-to-be. (It was a little later, probably in 1122, that Alexios, son of John and Irene, was also given a place, on a nearby pilaster.) This is a work of art of the highest quality, in which the creative genius of the artist who conceived it makes itself felt under many aspects.

Slightly higher than the others, the figure of the Virgin forms the central axis, strongly indicated in dark blue. Clad in gold, with blue and red glints in the folds, the Child forms a patch of radiant light against the blue of her cloak. Grave but strangely young, the Virgin's face is such as we see it in the best icons. Though there are reminiscences of the classical ideal of beauty in the features and proportions, the warm, delicate coloring of the face is obviously intended to appeal to the "inner eye" of the believer. For the Emperor and his wife were fervent Christians; that indeed is the message conveyed by this picture. But the artist realized that the presentation of living persons should, aesthetically, be differentiated from that of figures in an icon, and, despite the formalism of the official garments, the "human element" is stressed. This is one of the earliest intimations of the growing awareness of Byzantine artists that, while conservative methods were suitable for sacred images, the portrait called for a new approach. It is curious and perhaps significant that more concern for plastic values is evidenced in sacred images—the Virgin's in this case—than in portraits. As against the monumentalism of the figures in the panel beside it, the drawing of those of John and Irene is more flexible; there are even faint hints of the plastic qualities of bodies under the garments and in the folds of the *loros* on the emperor's arm. Whereas the money-bag held by Constantine IX is symmetrical, rigorously stylized, the top of John's is supple and drooping naturally. Garments are not treated as mere decorative passages independent of the figures, and this is why we do not get the effect of heads emerging from a carapace. But it is above all in the faces that the difference is manifest. In the second picture the mosaicist has handled his tesserae like so many tiny touches of color and employed them lavishly. Pinks, vivid greens and groupings of paler hues enable him delicately to build up faces, which he treats far more from the angle of the colorist than from that of the sculptor; thus he eschews the large tracts of shadow we find in the mosaic of the south vestibule. Contours mean much to him; the curve of Irene's face is nothing short of masterly. In each portrait the gaze is full of life and the lines of the mouth give the face an individuality that is enhanced by the distinctive color of the eyes (luminous grey in Irene's case) and the hair; John's is dark, Irene's fair. In the curls and tresses of the young empress's hair, treated as decorative elements, the artist has achieved a particularly happy effect. To similar effects, and to skillful alternations of graphic and chromatic arabesques, are due the shimmering planes of iridescent color in the royal robes of red and purple silk.

If I have stressed the differences between the two votive mosaics, this must not be taken to mean that an evolution on lines suggested by these works was taking place from the mid-eleventh century on. To correct any such impression, we need only turn to the oldest mosaic in the south vestibule; its style is far closer to that of the John-and-Irene mosaic than to that of the Constantine-and-Zoë panel. The truth is that these mosaics were turned out by workshops of differing traditions that, so far as we can judge, functioned side by side throughout the eleventh century and which, though certainly they kept in touch (as is shown by the simultaneous disappearance of broad shadows in all the mosaics in the gallery), took each its own path. We find the same thing happening in eleventh-century Greece, where the mosaics in the churches do not illustrate successive stages of an evolutionary process but stem from different traditions; nor, for that matter, do they exactly correspond to what we find at the same period in St Sophia.

But while from one church to another, or (as in St Sophia) from one panel to the other, we observe changes of taste and of technique, there is also evidence pointing in the other direction and showing the persistence of certain craftsmanly traditions and aesthetic attitudes. Thus in the same south gallery of St Sophia a remarkably fine twelfth-century Deesis (without portraits of emperors or a donor's name) is aesthetically affiliated to the John-and-Irene mosaic. Here the execution is still more meticulous, with an accent on the precision of the drawing, which, if perhaps a trifle finical, is admirable of its kind. Delicacy of modeling is carried to its highest pitch and the light streaks of color on faces have their justification; so tenuous are they that they do not (as in so many portraits by provincial imitators of the Byzantines) make furrows in the cheeks; and similarly the lights on the edges of faces and hands are attenuated almost to the point of imperceptibility. The noble quality of this art, which owes much to classical models, and is thus in the lineage of that of Daphni (see below), is also to be seen in the frequent use of half-tones and subdued colors for figures and garments. Such is the technical finesse of this mosaic that it all but dispenses with the effects peculiar to this form of art and approximates, rather, to painting proper, thus heralding the portable mosaics of the age of the Palaeologi (see below).

THE DESCENT INTO LIMBO. DETAIL: CHRIST. MID-ELEVENTH CENTURY.
MOSAIC, CHURCH OF THE NEA MONI, CHIOS.

THE CHURCH OF THE NEA MONI IN CHIOS

The mosaics in the church of the "Nea Moni" (New Monastery), built it is believed in the mid-eleventh century, are in the choir, the single nave and narthex. Though some of these mosaics have disappeared, the general lay-out and "program" of the sacred themes depicted can be discerned, and the cleaning operations now in progress are gradually bringing to view the great artistic merits and profound originality of these too-little-known works.

Like all eleventh-century decorations, that in Chios keeps to a limited range of subjects; beside the Pantocrator (lost), a Virgin in the Orans position, and a few angels and saints, are only fourteen scenes, all derived from the New Testament and depicting the chief incidents of the Gospel narrative, from the Annunciation to Pentecost. An examination of some details of these scenes will enable us to form an adequate idea of the art of the mosaicists of Chios.

The first thing to strike us is the exceptional austerity, verging on crudeness, of their presentation. The compositional rhythm is established solely by the figures, whose forms are angular, their garments harshly geometrical and so stiff that they look starched. So violent are the contrasts between highlights and shadows that one has the impression of an almost garish light illuminating heads, limbs and clothing. Large zones of shadow dapple cheeks as well as garments, and emphatic outlines circumscribe the brightly lit passages. There is a uniform gold background, except for the soil below; indeed even in his depiction of the hills rising behind the figures, the artist has contented himself with indicating their outlines only, on the gold ground.

Notable in *The Crucifixion* is the group of the three Marys at the foot of the Cross: three versions of the theme of a woman, her features convulsed with grief, making sorrowful gestures and clad in a long robe, with a mantle *(maphorion)* covering her head and shoulders. Here the geometrical treatment of the faces, the Virgin's especially, is bolder than in any other Byzantine work, and nowhere else have artists ventured to obscure with such heavy shadows such large tracts of faces. The three harmonies of two cognate colors in the costumes of the three Marys (two slightly variant shades of blue for the Virgin) show the Byzantine artists' tactful handling of color at its best.

On the other side of the Cross we see St John in tears, but it is above all the little centurion—a charming figure certainly destined to be given a favored place in all anthologies of mediaeval art—who holds our interest. Gesticulating excitedly, the small soldier is wonderfully alive; his cast of face and the way his hair is dressed suggest he is an Arab; his uniform gleams with all the colors of the rainbow. Once more we can but admire the daring of the Chios artist who placed this gay profusion of reds, blues and yellows beside the figure of the apostle, in which drawing, colors and expression concur in an effect of classical serenity. In both figures the hands are treated in the same manner; modeled by patches of color and geometrically regular as to the drawing. Thus it is clear that these two figures were made at the same time and that the differences between them, noted above, are due to the versatile imagination of the mosaicist.

THE CRUCIFIXION. DETAIL: THE THREE MARYS AT THE FOOT OF THE CROSS. MID-ELEVENTH CENTURY.
MOSAIC, CHURCH OF THE NEA MONI, CHIOS.

One cannot conceive of an artist with a keener zest for color than the Master of the *Descent into Limbo*. Here Christ has a distinctly oriental cast of face and blue hair, His raiment is of another shade of blue, ribboned with gold, and the cross He bears is mauve. Apart from some broad, dark shadows on face and neck the flesh tints are pale, almost white—thus making an effective contrast with the brown and red contours of the arms. In the same scene the treatment of the "protoplasts" Adam and Eve, whom Christ is rescuing from hell, is remarkably "expressionist," whilst the modeling of heads and hair, and two passages of drapery—one in warm and the other in cool hues—is no less effective. Here colors are relatively discreet as compared with those of the symmetrical group of the Kings of Israel risen from the dead. Blues, greens, reds, white and gold are skillfully intermingled and harmonize despite clashes of seemingly incongruous colors. We have here a work to which justice cannot be done in black-and-white photographic reproduction, and indeed this holds good for all the Chios mosaics, which owe so much to the artist's sensitive feeling for color and his skillful handling of it. Of landscape nothing has survived in the *Descent into Limbo* except the outlines of a golden hill and some arrow-shaped patches indicating jagged rocks. Obviously no symbolical significance should be attributed to these "arrows," curious though they are.

THE CRUCIFIXION. DETAIL: CENTURION AT THE FOOT OF THE CROSS. MID-ELEVENTH CENTURY. MOSAIC, CHURCH OF THE NEA MONI, CHIOS.

THE DESCENT INTO LIMBO. DETAIL: THE KINGS OF ISRAEL. MID-ELEVENTH CENTURY.
MOSAIC, CHURCH OF THE NEA MONI, CHIOS.

THE DESCENT INTO LIMBO. DETAIL: ADAM AND EVE. MID-ELEVENTH CENTURY.
MOSAIC, CHURCH OF THE NEA MONI, CHIOS.

113

CHRIST PANTOCRATOR. CA. 1100. MOSAIC IN THE DOME, CHURCH OF DAPHNI.

DAPHNI, NEAR ELEUSIS

Some fifty years intervened between the decorations in Chios and the more famous ones at Daphni, the latter being dated on good grounds to about 1100. Apart from the family likeness which, as is natural, we expect to find in works that belong to more or less the same period, there is very little in common between the art of Daphni and that of Chios, and I greatly question whether these two decorations should be regarded as representing successive phases in the evolution of the same species of art. In my opinion we have here two distinct schools of painting which, allowing for local differences, are paralleled by the two votive pictures in St Sophia: that of Constantine Monomachus and Zoë on the one hand, and that of John II and Irene Comnena on the other.

We have already pointed out with reference to the last-named mosaic and the neighboring Deesis (which not merely shows the same tendencies but carries them a stage farther) that the distinctive features of these twelfth-century works are the delicacy of the drawing and their classicizing forms. Probably slightly antedating those at St Sophia, the mosaics at Daphni are obviously conceived in the same spirit and employ much the same technical procedures, though it must be admitted that they fall short of the formal precision of the panels in the "Great Church." As against the dynamism of the Chios decorations and their dramatic boldness those at Daphni have the suave beauty of a humanistic Christian art. Indeed it is at Daphni that for the first time, chronologically speaking, we find the methods of classical art employed systematically and overtly in a Byzantine mural painting. (This time-lag as against the appearance of similar classicizing tendencies in the art of the miniature is perhaps surprising and certainly significant.) Undoubtedly these developments were far more a matter of the taste of individual schools than due to any widespread *renovatio* of classical art in progress at this time.

The iconographical arrangement at Daphni has a close resemblance to that in Chios and at St Luke's in Phocis. The Pantocrator lords it in the dome and the Virgin in the apse, while angels, prophets and saints figure on arches, vaults and niches, and finally, we have the usual eclectic group of Gospel scenes, of which there are thirteen in the nave and six in the narthex. It is the same cycle as in Chios, but the slight extension which is given here to scenes of Christ's Passion and the childhood of the Virgin fore-shadows the popularity of these subjects from the thirteenth century onward.

The Daphni *Nativity* is one of the peak-points of what might be termed the academic Byzantine style; it has much dignity, and its gracious, if somewhat facile beauty is classical in conception. Tactile values meant considerably more to the maker of this mosaic (this holds good for all the Daphni mosaics) than purely painterly values; indeed this style leads up to pictures looking like colored bas-reliefs and as solidly "built up" as actual sculpture. So self-sufficient and well-balanced is the composition of the various scenes that each may be regarded as an independent picture; nevertheless they fit in admirably and harmoniously with the over-all arrangement of the decoration. Thus in the *Nativity* a ray extending to the sky links up, aesthetically, the mosaic with the niche that shelters it.

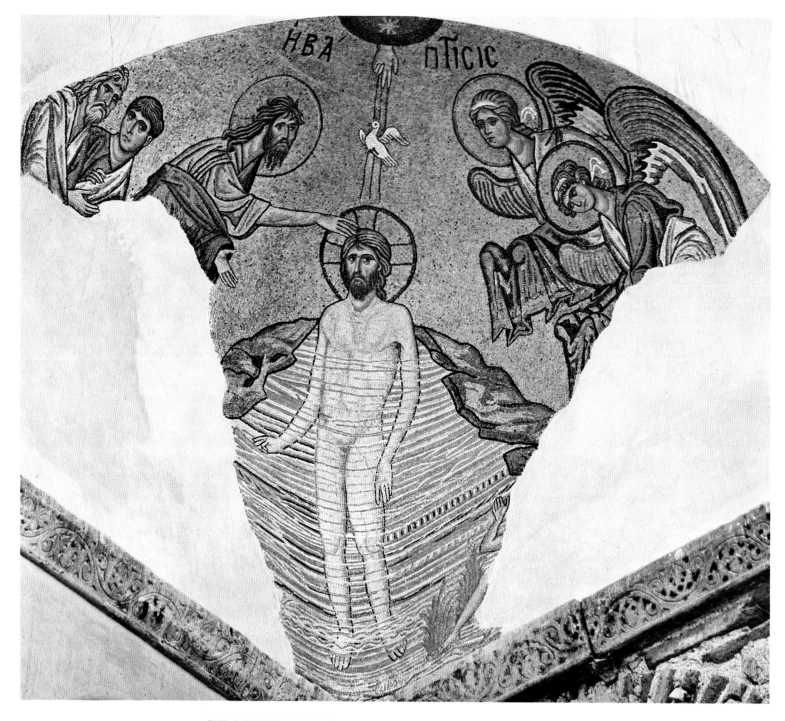

THE BAPTISM OF CHRIST. CA. 1100. MOSAIC IN THE NAVE, CHURCH OF DAPHNI.

In *The Baptism* the same function is assigned to the nude figure of Christ standing in the Jordan facing St John. This (like the figure of Christ in *The Crucifixion*, also at Daphni) may rank among the best of all Byzantine nudes: the forms are fuller than usual, the modeling is discreet but effective, while an unsymmetrical attitude at once

THE NATIVITY. CA. 1100. MOSAIC IN THE NAVE, CHURCH OF DAPHNI.

heightens the interest of the figure and gives the body stable poise. In the form of Christ as here depicted there is no trace of the mannerisms of the ascetic art that was coming into vogue during this period; and, like the apostles, the angels have plump, pink cheeks and comely faces.

All the Daphni mosaics bear the stamp of the academic Byzantine art of the epoch, with the sole exception of the central figure, the Pantocrator in the dome. Here one feels that the artist was of opinion that any display of academic elegance would be unseemly, and the grimness of the face—this forceful depiction is the least "amiable" of all Byzantine images of Christ—reminds us in some respects of the art of Chios. But the way in which the head is modeled, without surface shadows, and the filigree of thin lines upon the face have no equivalents in Chios; here we have a graphic technique somewhat akin to that of the Deēsis panel in St Sophia. The rather peculiar drawing of the hands may probably be due to the difficulties the mosaicist encountered when he sought to neutralize optical distortions due to the concave surface on which he had to work when designing the effigy in the cupola.

THE MOSAICS OF VENETIA

During the twelfth and thirteenth centuries many churches on the Italian coast of the Adriatic were decorated with mosaics that were either Byzantine or in the Byzantine manner, though made by local artists. The largest and handsomest are at Venice and Torcello, but there are others at Murano, Trieste and Ravenna. The fact that all these works are more or less akin points to the existence in this part of Italy, probably at Venice, of active schools of mosaic-workers practicing Byzantine techniques and methods. None the less a discrepancy between the mosaics made in the Venetian area and truly Byzantine mosaics makes itself felt in varying degrees, particularly at Venice itself, in most of the mosaics in the nave of St Mark's. This is why no example of that famous group of mosaics figures in the present volume, which is devoted to Byzantine art in the strict sense of the term. As regards St Mark's, however, we make one exception: in favor of the mosaics in the north narthex. They have a twofold interest for the student of Byzantine art, since not only were they directly inspired by sixth-century Byzantine miniatures, but the methods employed for the narrative scenes in this thirteenth-century decoration resemble those of the contemporary Greek and Serbian artists whose works we reproduce.

TORCELLO

Nevertheless it is in Torcello, in the huge basilica that was erected in the eleventh century on the island bearing that name in the Venetian lagoon, that we find mosaics most closely approximating to Byzantine originals. Moreover two of the works still to be seen in the basilica are not only masterpieces but round off our knowledge of authentically Byzantine art, as it was in the Middle Ages, to the happiest effect.

When it was originally built the basilica was decorated with frescos only, and some large fragments of painting (figures of saints) are still to be seen beneath the mosaics in the apse. The style of these paintings is quite unmistakably that of eleventh-century Byzantine art. The mosaics were put in later, in the course of the twelfth century. It was then that there was made that famous effigy of the Virgin, towering above the apostles, which seems to float serenely in a great sea of golden light. The exceptionally grandiose effect of this decoration is due for the most part to the vastness of the surface assigned to gold alone. This is a typically Byzantine procedure. No other mediaeval artists dared to employ empty spaces as a means of aesthetic expression so freely and to such dramatic effect as the Byzantines. But it was the Torcello mosaicist who, greatly daring, turned this procedure to most spectacular account, and he achieved this by eliminating the figures of the saints or angels usually placed beside the Virgin in the apses of churches, and also by depicting the Mother of God herself as a slender, delicately built young woman.

Facing this celestial vision, on the west wall of the basilica, is an immense depiction of the *Last Judgment*, and this is no less famous and typically Byzantine than the mosaics in the apse. On the highest register of the wall is a *Crucifixion*, below it the *Resurrection*, and underneath there comes this superb picture of the Second Coming and the Last Judgment. It took the Church many centuries to compile the iconographical

THE LAST JUDGMENT. FRAGMENT: SINNERS IN HELL. TWELFTH CENTURY. MOSAIC, BASILICA, TORCELLO.

VIRGIN AND CHILD. TWELFTH CENTURY. MOSAIC IN THE APSE,
BASILICA, TORCELLO.

data for the representation of the Last Day under its numerous awe-inspiring, comminatory and didactic aspects, and at Torcello we have not only one of the earliest but also one of the fullest versions of the scene. The component parts of this vision of Judgment have different origins—which explains why they are handled on different lines; thus alongside groups of august figures inspired by ceremonies of the Church and Court, we find scenes and figures on which the artists gave rein to their natural inventiveness and personal imagination. They allowed themselves most scope in picturing the retribution of the wicked; as in the fragment here reproduced, with its little blue devils who seem to be playing ball with the heads of Christ's enemies—an emperor, Mohammed, a mustachioed heathen chief, a bishop, some princesses—all alike doomed to the quenchless fire.

VENICE: ST MARK'S

As already mentioned, the mosaics at St Mark's (like the other mosaics in Venetia) were not the work of Byzantine artists, as indeed is evidenced, more or less clearly, by their style. Nevertheless Venetian disciples of the Greeks kept in contact with Constantinople over a long period, and aligned their art to its successive manners. Thus while the artists working on the nave of St Mark's obviously drew inspiration from Byzantine models of not later than the twelfth century, the thirteenth-century decorations in the narthex, which are modeled on one of the contemporary cycles of biblical anecdotes, reflect the new tendencies of the decorators of Byzantine churches during the same period. Moreover, it has been proved that the makers of the mosaics in the narthex took for their models the Greek illustrations in a sixth-century Bible (similar to the "Cottonian" Bible in the British Museum) and probably their Byzantine and Serbian

THE MIRACLE OF THE QUAILS. EXODUS SEQUENCE. THIRTEENTH CENTURY. MOSAIC, ST MARK'S, VENICE.

contemporaries followed the same course when commissioned to decorate church walls with similar sets of narrative pictures on biblical themes.

By way of this return to Early Christian sources at both Byzantium and Venice artists were brought into contact with many reminiscences of classical art. Moreover, the anecdotal nature of these pictures gave them opportunities of introducing—whether purposely or not—concrete facts of visual experience and of giving their art a bias towards nature-imitation. Thus in the mosaics of the narthex at St Mark's we find the typical Hellenistic landscape of hills and decorative buildings reappearing; also many motifs which, following a practice of the close of classical Antiquity, introduce touches of local color (e.g. camels, pyramids) into anecdotal scenes. But we also find a host of deviations from the classical Greek models; for the Italian artists were far from being slavish imitators and, without playing false to the spirit of the older works, enlivened and enriched them with their personal observations of men and things.

We see this process at work in the two scenes of miracles (as described in Exodus XVI, XVII): the quails that "at even came up and covered the camp" to feed the children of Israel in the desert, and the water miraculously gushing forth to quench their thirst, with Moses praying for them under the starry night-sky. This art shows an advance on that of the mosaics in Sicily (see following chapter) in the direction of greater realism as to details (e.g. the woman roasting the quails), which, moreover, are no longer precisely in the Byzantine spirit.

VAULT MOSAIC. TWELFTH CENTURY. CATHEDRAL OF CEFALÙ.

THE MOSAICS OF SICILY

The mosaic church decorations commissioned by the Norman kings of Sicily in the twelfth century are the largest that exist. And since they reflect the style that was flourishing in Constantinople during the same period, we include here several reproductions of these mosaics. However, we must bear in mind the fact that the Sicilian mosaics were made far from Byzantium and local craftsmen played a more or less considerable part in their execution; also that in some measure they were affected by the immediate influence of the Western and even Islamic forms of art which then were simultaneously in favor at the Norman court.

For, nothing if not eclectic in their tastes, these kings patronized all forms of art alike, taking from each the qualities in which it most excelled. Thus the architecture of the Palatine Chapel was on Roman lines, the walls were lined with Byzantine mosaics, and the nave had a wooden "stalactite" ceiling combined with Moorish painting. But this eclecticism was not due solely to the fact that the Norman kings had no decided preferences in art; before their coming, Latin, Byzantine and Islamic art traditions had flourished side by side in Southern Italy and Sicily, and the Norman kings were merely adapting themselves to the *status quo* when they patronized impartially all three forms of art. Moreover there were special reasons why the Byzantine style of church decoration—sponsored by the Palermo and Cefalù mosaics—should have held its ground better in Sicily than in other regions of the West, since Sicily had been abandoned by the Eastern Empire only in the mid-ninth century, while other territories of the Norman kings in Southern Italy had remained Byzantine until the Norman conquest. In short, the art that flourished in Sicily at the time of the conquest—and of the foundation of the churches which were given mosaic decorations—was predominantly Byzantine, with some tincture of Islamic influence.

Thus it was only natural there should be a considerable Byzantine element in the art favored by the Norman kings of Sicily. But there was another reason, and a weighty one, for this: a matter of prestige. Since the Norman kings deliberately set out to vie with the basileis of the East, they tended instinctively to model not only the liveries, ceremonies and etiquette of their court, but also the mosaics in their churches on those of the Eastern capital.

★

As usually happened in the lands of Western Europe, Byzantine influences in Southern Italy during the Norman régime made themselves felt most strongly and persistently in the field of Christian iconography. Byzantium still possessed the most copious repertory of religious images and, despite the official separation of the Churches of Rome and Constantinople (in 1054), these had lost nothing of their renown, and the schism did not prevent either Desiderius (at Monte Cassino) or the Norman island kings from employing Byzantine artists.

CEFALÙ: THE CATHEDRAL

The mosaics in the cathedral at Cefalù (near Palermo), due to the munificence of King Roger II, were begun in 1148 and executed by groups of craftsmen under Greek supervision. Here the style is purely Byzantine, with this difference: that the dimensions of the edifice to be adorned with mosaics exceeded those of Byzantine churches and the structural plan—that of a basilica—necessitated certain modifications in the arrangement of the decorations. And since the lay-out of the frescos or mosaics in a Byzantine church always followed a set system, these deviations catch the eye at once. None the less, taken singly, all the pictures at Cefalù are in the purest style of Comnenian art.

The huge Pantocrator in the apse is the work of a very great artist. Despite an emphasis on linear pattern, there is far more here than mere calligraphy, notable being the finely balanced structure of the figure, with a *contrapposto* of the hands, one raised, the other clasped on the book it holds towards us; the sweeping movement of the right hand, implemented by the billowing drapery of the mantle; the immobility of the left, stressed by the vertical lines and ruffled edges of the garment. The same majestic, tranquil rhythm pervades the face of Christ, whose grave beauty corresponds exactly to that "image of God" which Greek post-iconoclast theologians bade artists realize in Christ's features, and whose function was to express the divine "energy" immanent in icons of the Son of God. But it is also the image of Christ the King, ruler of the universe, and this is why He towers above the other figures and the whole church is overshadowed by his gigantic presence.

For He is greater than the Virgin, the angels and (naturally) the apostles who figure in two successive tiers on the walls of the apse, beneath the Pantocrator. Nevertheless, as if to remind us that the Mother of God takes precedence of all the hierarchies of the world, archangels clad like emperors and wielding the imperial *labarum* and globe are paying homage to her—their attitudes and gestures make this clear—like princes paying homage to their suzerain. On the other hand, as if to emphasize the incompatibility between divine and worldly hierarchies, the Virgin, Queen of Heaven, displays no outward attributes of power, but is clad very simply in a long ungarnished robe and monochrome mantle, and the same is true of the Pantocrator, though some glints of gold dapple his garment.

Here the Virgin, shown in the attitude of oblation, though worshipped by angels and attended by apostles, is but the servant of God, a willing instrument of divine Providence. But in the apse at Cefalù she is placed in the midst of and above the human figures, in a position making her at once an intercessor between mankind and Christ and a living symbol of the Church. The artist who made the Cefalù mosaics was familiar with the esoteric language of contemporary Byzantine art (i.e. the inner significance of certain gestures, costumes and attributes), a language which differed from that of the parallel art manifestations of Western Europe in that figures of saints with a few objects beside them sufficed to convey to the beholder highly abstract concepts, and that thus the Byzantine artist did not need to resort to geometric patterns or personifications.

CHRIST PANTOCRATOR. TWELFTH CENTURY. MOSAIC IN THE APSE,
CATHEDRAL OF CEFALÙ.

(Thus, too, the buttresses of Byzantine domes are never on the exterior of buildings, their function being performed by interior pillars and side walls.) Obviously this special language of Byzantine art called for extreme distinctness and flawless precision in the drawing, and here, in fact, we have one of the great merits of Byzantine painting under the Macedonian and Comnenian dynasties. Everything is clean-cut, pellucid: outlines of figures, features, the few time-honored gestures and also the great empty spaces, so rare in mediaeval art, which at once set the rhythm of the composition and absorb into their all-pervading golden sheen alike the vividest and the most delicate patches of color. A perfect illustration is one of the small vaults at Cefalù, in which from the summits of the arches done in cool colors—white, blue and gold—to the ethereal faces of the angels, we find a soaring vision of transcendence seconded by consummate craftsmanship.

For this art attains a perfection all its own in the celestial visions of the vaults, the slow cortège of all-but-identical figures in the friezes, and the scenes in which figures, hills and buildings, sublimated from the material world, merge in an harmonious whole, built up by a rhythmic interplay of lines and masses.

PALERMO: THE PALATINE CHAPEL

The chapel of the king's palace at Palermo was likewise the work of Roger II. Founded in 1132 and consecrated in 1140, it is one of the handsomest sacred edifices of the Middle Ages, and in it an assemblage of seemingly incongruous elements produces, strangely enough, an effect of sumptuous, harmonious unity. Mosaics on the walls and vaults play the leading part in its interior decoration and here again, as at Cefalù, the art behind these pictures—all of sacred subjects—is wholly Byzantine. True, some of the figures have been identified as those of Western saints included at the instance of the Norman king, whose influence is even more apparent in the choice of certain themes and their location. Yet even here both inspiration and execution are Byzantine, and the only places in which this fidelity to Byzantine models is—to some slight extent—departed from are the naves, for whose mosaics Greek churches provided no exact equivalents.

Noteworthy amongst the works in which Byzantine art of the period of the Comneni can be seen at its purest is the sequence of "Fathers of the Church," and in particular the portrait (alongside that of St Basil the Great) of St John Chrysostom. The vast dome of the forehead, edged with a narrow strip of hair, is skillfully suggested by a slightly oblique circle and two finely drawn arcs, while two curving, white-rimmed lines extend from cheeks to chin, and the hollows below the cheeks are indicated by bracketed half-crescents. The mouth is fully modeled, whereas the ears are mere abstract signs, and jet-black eyes under craggy brows make an effective contrast with the soft tones of the face. There is an almost spectral quality in this portrait, and the emaciation of the face and its faraway gaze suggest that the Byzantine artist aimed at depicting the great fourth-century orator and theologian as an ascetic visionary. The geometrical treatment of the Saint's garments, the crosses, the book and hand, and the thin red outline of the

ST BASIL THE GREAT AND ST JOHN CHRYSOSTOM. TWELFTH CENTURY.
MOSAIC, PALATINE CHAPEL, PALERMO.

THE NATIVITY. TWELFTH CENTURY. MOSAIC, PALATINE CHAPEL, PALERMO.

nimbus contribute to this effect of vigorous expressionism implemented by an exceptionally bold interpretation of physical reality. There is a world of difference between this ascetic vision of St John Chrysostom and his tenth-century portrait in St Sophia.

In *The Entrance into Jerusalem*, one of the large compositions in the Palatine Chapel, we have an excellent example of the Byzantine art of this period. The subject is one which enabled Christian artists (beginning in the sixth century at the latest) to employ formulas of imperial art without diverging from the Gospel text. At Palermo too—and perhaps Roger II and his court insisted on this, the king having been likened to Christ—Jesus is shown making a triumphal entry into His city, acclaimed by the populace. Here the pattern of an imperial "triumph" is adjusted to the Gospel narrative;

THE ENTRANCE INTO JERUSALEM. TWELFTH CENTURY. MOSAIC, PALATINE CHAPEL, PALERMO.

thus Christ is riding *downhill* towards the city, He is attended by the apostles, the city fathers welcoming Him have the look and attire of orientals, while haloes remind us of the sanctity of many of the figures.

But the chief contribution made by the Byzantines of the Middle Ages to this stock theme—and doubtless the source of its popularity—was the clarity and skill with which its sacred implications were presented. The conventions of their art enabled them to disregard the space dimension and, as here, to detach the main group of figures from the decorative group of children, placed like a charming predella, under Christ's feet. The city of Jerusalem is moved down to the lowest register, but the welcoming crowd occupies a small raised dais led up to by three steps. There was, obviously, no factual justification for the dais, but it served to place the group at a suitable level as regards that of Christ, and at the far end of a curve indicating at once the hierarchic status of those present—Christ, St Peter, the other apostles, the people of Jerusalem—and the general movement of the composition. The procession is descending a hill, but the gradient is suggested not by the positions assigned the figures (this might have impaired the majesty of the triumphal Entrance) but by the crest-lines of successive hillsides. In the case of St Peter this produces a curious effect; he seems to be stepping on two hills at once and unaware of the fact that the ass's hoof is crushing his big toe. On the other hand, the relative positions of St Peter and the palm-tree and the parallelism between the front part of the apostle's body and that of Christ play an important part in the composition; the figures of Christ and the apostle form its focal point, both spiritual and aesthetic, while the turned head of the apostle and the gaze of the disciple heading the group behind their Master guide the spectator's eye towards the face of Christ the King making His triumphal entry.

Each of the other scenes in the Chapel would repay detailed study on these lines. The *Nativity* we reproduce, while as happily inspired and skillfully handled as the others, is one of the most impressive, owing to the sensuous richness of the colors. Greens, ochres, softly iridescent pearly hues, interspersed with passages of white and sudden glints of gold, form color harmonies of a rare and memorable beauty.

THE ENROLLMENT FOR TAXATION BEFORE CYRENIUS. FOURTEENTH CENTURY. MOSAIC IN A LUNETTE.
OUTER NARTHEX, KAHRIEH DJAMI, CONSTANTINOPLE.

CONSTANTINOPLE
THE CHURCH OF KAHRIEH DJAMI

Two centuries intervened between the making of the Daphni mosaics and the decoration of the two vestibules of the small church at Constantinople commonly known under its Turkish name, Kahrieh Djami. Originally the church of the " Monastery of Christ of Chora" (i.e. "Christ-in-the-Fields"), this is a very ancient edifice and each narthex—there are two—was decorated with mosaics in the first years of the fourteenth century, thanks to the enlightened munificence of a cultured Court dignitary, Theodore Metochita.

PEACOCK. FOURTEENTH CENTURY. DETAIL. MOSAIC IN A PENDENTIVE.
INNER NARTHEX, KAHRIEH DJAMI, CONSTANTINOPLE.

These mosaics comprise an exceptionally large number of pictures, including many figures of Christ, the Virgin and Saints, as well as a prodigious diversity of ornamental work. Indeed, the wealth of purely decorative elements in Kahrieh Djami is paralleled only in the fifth-century churches of Salonica and Ravenna. The artists engaged by Metochita had probably inspected, and admired, these gorgeous Early Christian decorations, and that fervent humanist, the donor, could but approve of the imitation of ancient models. That models of this kind, much like those inspiring the makers of the Daphni mosaics, were here employed is suggested by the pictures of several isolated saints and particularly by the treatment of the head in the portrait of a martyr-saint here reproduced. The whole figure is a masterpiece of subtle artistry; singularly attractive is this fair-haired youth, like a mediaeval page, who wears so becomingly his raiment of light silk picked out with gold and holds with equal elegance his ceremonial sword and the martyr's cross. The color-scheme in delicate blues and greens, and even the gleams of gold upon the young saint's costume, have the same elegant refinement, a refinement that had never yet been attained in the long history of Byzantine art. Thus at the selfsame time when the storm clouds were gathering over Constantinople, and the pressure of stern reality was growing ever more insistent, the artists took to conjuring up dreams of an exquisitely fragile beauty.

THE CITY OF NAZARETH. FOURTEENTH CENTURY. DETAIL. MOSAIC IN A LUNETTE.
OUTER NARTHEX, KAHRIEH DJAMI, CONSTANTINOPLE.

A MARTYR-SAINT. FOURTEENTH CENTURY. MOSAIC. OUTER NARTHEX,
KAHRIEH DJAMI, CONSTANTINOPLE.

We find similar tendencies in the two sets of Gospel scenes which form the bulk of the decorations at Kahrieh Djami and, in the vestibules, depict the Childhood of Christ preceded by the story of his Mother, and the miracles—subjects, that is to say, which from the strictly theological viewpoint were secondary; the leading Gospel themes being reserved for the nave (these decorations no longer exist at Kahrieh Djami). True, most of the narratives illustrated here are apocryphal, but the Church always permitted their use. However, they were not equally appreciated everywhere and always; after an early vogue in the sixth century (e.g. the frescos at Perustica in Thrace), their popularity waned, and it was only from the thirteenth century on, under the Palaeologi, that they returned to favor. The fresco-painters of the period of the Kahrieh Djami mosaics often

THE JOURNEY TO BETHLEHEM. FOURTEENTH CENTURY. MOSAIC IN A LUNETTE.
OUTER NARTHEX, KAHRIEH DJAMI, CONSTANTINOPLE.

reverted to themes dealing with the life of the Virgin and the Childhood of Christ; indeed all the artists of this late phase of Byzantine art tended to hark back to the iconography of the past. The human interest of these subjects made it easier to interpolate realistic motifs and picturesque variations of the time-honored formulas, while their homelier appeal quickened the artist's personal emotions, and these were reflected in his work.

Both the new tendencies can be seen in the Kahrieh Djami frescos. These are scenes in which the quest of picturesque and anecdotal effects predominates, leading the artist to amplify the content of his pictures. That of *The Enrollment for Taxation* (i.e. the census described in Luke II) is a case in point. The number of Roman officials shown beside Joseph and Mary, the costumes, weapons, coiffures, the considerable space allotted to queer-looking trees and buildings—everything here is the work of an artist of high originality who, greatly daring, gave a definitely baroque twist to his versions of Byzantine themes.

Unlike him, the artists responsible for the other panels are more cautious in their use of baroque devices. This discretion is evidenced by the artist's handling of the garments of the leading figures and the slight elongation of Joseph's body in the *Journey to Bethlehem*. His aim is to express the subtle, almost nostalgic emotions that mysterious journey inspired in him, and to this end much use is made of creamy yellows and a wide range of softly luminous greys, forming a background to the frail, poignant beauty of the Virgin. Silently the little cortège moves across the scene, laden with the hopes of a world awaiting its Savior's birth. Thus along with baroque tendencies the Kahrieh Djami artists cultivated a poetic, even sentimental approach to their subjects; they, too, aimed at interpreting reality, but a reality of the heart rather than that of concrete visual experience.

Furthermore, all these artists had a way of combining religious themes with lighter, purely pleasure-giving motifs, details that often have a singular charm. Thus sometimes, on the outskirts of a scene, we see an ancient city, whose small, many-colored houses are bathed in gay Mediterranean sunlight; or, again, there may be playful *putti* or some stately peacock raising, without unfurling, its iridescent plumage glittering with flakes of gold.

FRESCOS IN THE BALKANS AND GREECE
ELEVENTH TO FOURTEENTH CENTURY

Though there was no order to this effect in the edicts of any Council, every Byzantine church, after the passing of Iconoclasm, was adorned with iconographical pictures. Covering all the surfaces available within the church, they usually were made at the time of its foundation. In fact every time a church was built the skilled artist's cooperation was considered indispensable. This was never the case in Western Europe, numerous as were the murals in Romanesque and pre-Romanesque churches. To account for the proliferation of mural painting in Byzantium, we would remind the reader of a fact already noted in our Introduction: that, from the ninth century on, the iconographical decorations of Byzantine churches formed a coherent, more or less fixed compendium of Christian symbols which, in virtue of their content and emplacement, linked up functionally both with the edifice itself and with the rites performed within it. The paintings, in fact, were complementary to the church services, and gave visual explanations of them.

From the religious viewpoint, both mosaics and frescos were equally suitable for the depiction of the required symbols. But the costliness of the mosaic process often led to the use of the mural paintings we describe as "frescos" in the present work, without distinguishing between true *a fresco* painting (i.e. with *all* the pigments applied while the wall is still wet) and the kind of painting that combines *buon fresco* technique with another (some of the pigments being applied *a secco* on a ground of local colors previously laid in *a fresco*). Long practice made the Byzantine artist expert in the art of painting walls and vaults, indeed one feels he was never at a loss for suitable procedures; but while this ensured a rare perfection as to style, it also involved, inevitably, the frequent use of pictorial *clichés*.

CHURCHES IN JUGOSLAVIA

Theoretically, a study of mediaeval frescos should begin with works of the period immediately following the downfall of Iconoclasm. But, except for a few fragments, no ninth- or tenth-century frescos have survived, and we have no option but to begin with a work—which, as it so happens, is of the very highest quality—ascribed to the first half of the eleventh century, and figuring in the Cathedral of St Sophia at Ochrid (Jugoslavian Macedonia), an important religious center of the period. These frescos, some of which have been uncovered only since the second World War, keep to the usual lay-out of eleventh-century Byzantine decorations (cf. Chios and Daphni), and though their style is more flexible than that of the mosaics, certain fragments are remarkable for the schematism of their rigid, abstract imaging. The scene in the choir, depicting

CATHEDRAL OF ST SOPHIA, OCHRID

ST BASIL. ELEVENTH CENTURY. FRESCO IN THE CHOIR, CATHEDRAL OF ST SOPHIA, OCHRID.
Copyright by the Federal Institute for the Preservation of Historical Monuments, Belgrade.

St Basil officiating at the Mass, is a noteworthy example; the artist has kept the painting flat throughout, paten and eucharistic bread are depicted vertically as if they stood on end, and the marble pavement as if making a straight line with the wall behind. Here we see the Byzantine fresco style at its severest and most formal.

It was a style that lasted longer than might have been expected; indeed we find conservative painters still employing it in the twelfth century. But during the same period (that of the Comneni) other artists, endowed with greater sensibility, gave the art of the fresco a new direction, imparting to it both flexibility and expressiveness. Vibrant with life and sometimes deeply moving, these frescos—which belong to the second half of the twelfth century—are in advance of all European paintings of the same period. The decoration in the Church of Nerezi near Skoplje (Jugoslavia) is one of the two masterpieces of this art, the other, later by some decades, being in the Cathedral of St Demetrios at Vladimir (Russia). The Nerezi frescos have the advantage of being dated (1164), but as usual nothing is known of the artist or artists responsible for them, though the inscription tells us, besides the date, that they were commissioned by a member of the family of the Comneni.

Though some scenes are missing, the iconographic program of the Nerezi frescos can be reconstructed in its broad lines, and it then becomes evident that the cycle of themes and concepts it incorporates had changed but little since the eleventh century. Only a few scenes of the Passion—the Descent from the Cross, the Entombment, and the Mourning of the Virgin—have been added to the leading episodes of the Gospel narrative, and pictured, in large, in the most conspicuous places. As regards style, however, the position is very different and these paintings strike a new note. Thus in the row of portraits of saints at the foot of the walls we have a pageant of living figures with individualized faces and a "speaking" gaze, while in the Gospel scenes, also, the new conception of art makes itself felt in various ways.

What could be more impressive than the figure of the young apostle in the *Transfiguration*, stricken down by the light of the Theophany, his eyes still aglow with memories of the supernal vision? Admirable, too, is the composition of the front part of his body and the arms enframing his head—a powerfully expressive face emerging from a triangle of drapery.

Or let us turn to the scene of a neighbor bringing St Anne some warm food in a globe-shaped utensil. Her head is slightly turned and her profile shows up, clean-cut as the effigy on an ancient coin, against the open door. True, there are classical reminiscences in the drawing and supple modeling of the head and in the sensuous fullness and movement of the arms, but these have been revivified by observation of reality.

In the *Entrance into Jerusalem* the artist went further in the direction of literal truth to life; costumes, headdresses and even the racial types portrayed show that he wished to give a realistic rendering of Oriental Semites in the group of Jews waiting at the city gate. Thus here it was in the guise of ethnical local color that traditional iconography was vitalized by contact with reality. But it was the episodes of the Passion

THE ENTRANCE INTO JERUSALEM. DETAIL: GROUP OF FIGURES. 1164. FRESCO, CHURCH OF NEREZI.

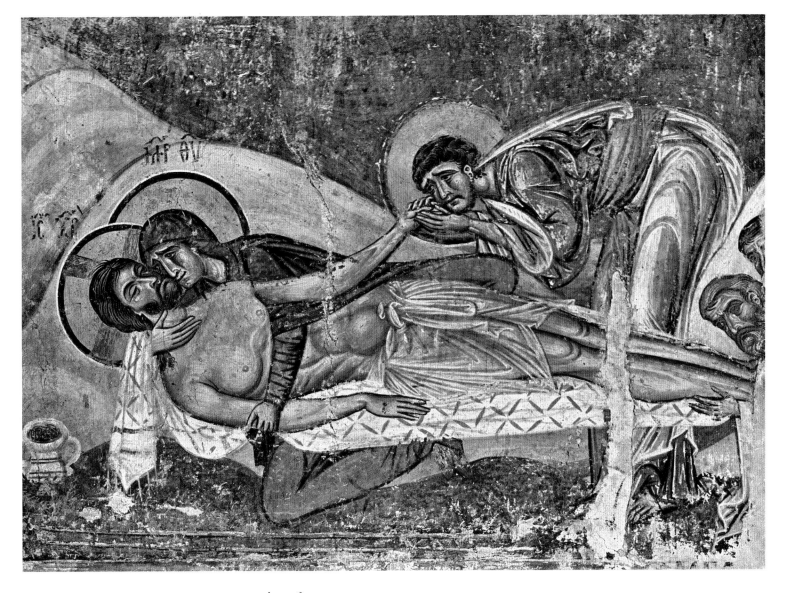

PIETÀ. 1164. FRESCO, CHURCH OF NEREZI.

and their scenes of death and suffering that, above all, stirred the Nerezi painter to a closer observation of nature and particularly of the movements, gestures and demeanor of a human being racked by pain or moved by deep compassion. Indeed, the Nerezi *Pietà* (dated 1164) constitutes a landmark in the history of European painting.

About 1235 Vladislav, King of the Serbs, had the Monastery Church of Milesevo built and decorated with paintings at his expense, amongst the paintings being a portrait of himself, as donor. Neither the founder of this church nor, probably, the artists he employed were Greeks, as had been the case at Nerezi and Ochrid. In fact we here have the work of native-born Serbians (and this holds good also for other churches in Jugoslavia, discussed below). Nevertheless these paintings illustrate certain stages in the

MONASTERY CHURCH OF MILESEVO

143

development of Byzantine art: stages of which otherwise we should know next to nothing owing to the dearth of works that have survived in lands within the Greek area. Thus some of the work produced in local workshops, thanks to the wealth and munificence of the Serbian kings, is valuable to us for the light it throws on the art of the Orthodox Byzantine world as a whole.

The Milesevo painters took over the procedures inaugurated at Nerezi, but carried them farther. While making the most of "picturesque" details and of "local color," they also gave a special emphasis to plastic values and modeling, and were particularly successful in their treatment of the human body and of garments. This new awareness of weight and volume even led them to exaggerate these; their figures are massive, ponderous, usually immobile. By way of Early Christian mosaics (at Salonica?) these fresco-painters had come in contact with certain aspects of the classical tradition, and they turned this

THE TRANSFIGURATION. DETAIL: APOSTLE. 1164. FRESCO, CHURCH OF NEREZI.

THE BIRTH OF THE VIRGIN. DETAIL: WOMAN CARRYING A UTENSIL. 1164. FRESCO, CHURCH OF NEREZI.

THE RESURRECTION. DETAIL: ANGEL. CA. 1235. FRESCO, CHURCH OF MILESEVO.

VLADISLAV, KING OF THE SERBS. CA. 1235. FRESCO, CHURCH OF MILESEVO.

THE DORMITION OF THE VIRGIN. FRAGMENT: GROUP OF APOSTLES. CA. 1265. FRESCO, CHURCH OF SOPOCANI.

THE DORMITION OF THE VIRGIN. CA. 1320. FRESCO, CHURCH OF GRACANICA.

knowledge to good account. These classicizing tendencies can be seen in the *Angel of the Resurrection*, but no less notable are the wealth of color in the body and the broad, heavily charged brushstrokes.

Like the twelfth-century mosaicist at St Sophia, Constantinople, who employed different procedures for his depiction of the Virgin and for that of the Emperors, the Milesevo painters used for the portrait of the monarch (ca. 1235) a style and technique differing from those they used for their religious images. The trend of this painting was frankly realistic and it too, like the Nerezi *Pietà*, constitutes a landmark in the history of European painting and of the European portrait in particular. Our plate, which brings out each individual brushstroke, also shows that in the vigorous modeling of Vladislav's face the artist has omitted the greenish-grey shading employed for modeling the faces

ST JOHN THE BAPTIST. CA. 1320. DETAIL. FRESCO, CHURCH OF GRACANICA.

of the angel and the saints. This distinction between the artistic expression of the two kinds of reality, material and spiritual, seems to have originated in the twelfth century. But it was not until the thirteenth—at Milesevo, at Boiana (Bulgaria) and in some miniatures (e.g. the *Typicon* at Lincoln College, Oxford)—that it was pressed to its logical conclusion, the result being some surprisingly vivacious portraits.

The Serbian painters of the next generation can be seen at their best in the decorations at Sopocani (ca. 1265); these fine frescos (which unhappily are threatened with progressive deterioration due to moisture) certainly deserve a leading place in every anthology of thirteenth-century pre-Renaissance art. At Sopocani, a foundation of the royal family of Serbia, we have one of the earliest examples—prior to Kahrieh Djami—of a complex decorative scheme in which several different cycles of pictures are brought together, and the iconographical program is far more copious than in the early period. But what commands our admiration is, above all, the rare quality of the painting. This can be seen to advantage in details of the huge *Dormition of the Virgin* on the west wall of the nave. Here, as at Milesevo, what instantly impresses us is the artist's feeling for grandiose effect, and the dignity of the draped figure. The bearded apostles beside the couch remind us of philosophers of Antiquity and the rhythm imparted to their movement is as clearly inspired by classical art as is the drawing of the garments and the ample modeling of bodies. It was from the same models that these artists learnt the secret of giving their figures stable poise and planting their feet solidly on the ground. If we wish to gauge the distance covered in two centuries, it is well to turn back to the Ochrid frescos, in which the figures seem almost to float in air, without any foothold on *terra firma*. The same classical inspiration (due probably to observation of ancient statuary) and the same predilection for thick, robust forms can be seen in the background architecture: big pilasters, columns of veined marble, capitals, cornices—all forming a solid block behind the figures, and a clearly defined spatial context for the scene of the Dormition. In the Sopocani fresco we have certainly the most brilliant example of what thirteenth-century artists achieved by way of a return to nature, making the procedures of classical Byzantine art their starting-point.

The circumstances which led this innovating movement to be cut short in Serbia shortly after 1300 were identical with those which had a similar effect in Byzantium and all the Orthodox lands, and there is no need to recapitulate them here. There was a reversion to academicism, either mannered or baroque, and more in line with the traditional procedures of Byzantine art. From the fourteenth century on, this style, which had been foreshadowed by the Kahrieh Djami mosaics, prevailed in all parts of the Byzantine world. At Nagoricino and a little later at Gracanica (both in Serbia) this was the style employed at the beginning of the century for all large-scale decorations containing various scenes and numerous figures.

In the Gracanica frescos (ca. 1320) the creative verve as well as the great skill of some of the artists working on them is unmistakable. We find both these qualities in the

Dormition, which, according to the so-called "complementary system" of iconography, combines the death of the Virgin with the scene of her body being borne away by the Apostles. Here the painters' indebtedness to the art of the previous generation, as illustrated at Sopocani, is patent. But this very similarity enables us to see how much has been lost: above all that quality which gave the Sopocani frescos their exceptional charm—the freshness of a new approach to art inspired at once by classical Antiquity and by observation of reality. Though, at Gracanica and elsewhere, fourteenth-century painters utilize the same forms and motifs as the Sopocani artists, they seem to have lost the "personal touch" and the first fine rapture of the pioneer; they are as indifferent to humanism as to nature imitation. True, the *Dormition of the Virgin* at Gracanica is painted in rich, warm colors, with many figures, and the over-all effect is vivacious, not to say dramatic; but its merits are mainly of a formal order: arrangements of masses and colors, harmonies of delicate hues, emotional expressions on faces.

On a close-up view it is perhaps the sheer virtuosity of the painter of *St John the Baptist* that strikes us most. But remarkable as is the sparing use of color, it is above all a fine example of what might be described as "iconographic calligraphy," as perfect in its way and often as otherworldly in effect as a hagiographical piece by Symeon Metaphrastes or his post-tenth-century imitators.

CHURCHES AT MISTRA

Meanwhile on the Greek mainland the despots of Morea were building churches in their capital, Mistra, and decorating them with frescos. These belong to the same period (thirteenth, fourteenth, fifteenth centuries) and sometimes, but not always, show the same inspiration as the Serbian frescos. It was at Mistra that half a century ago Gabriel Millet made the discovery of the beauties of Late Byzantine frescos and embarked on his great study of "The Renaissance under the Palaeologi." Unfortunately, since then the Mistra paintings have suffered the ravages of time, some are now quite ruined and

GROUP OF MARTYRS. FOURTEENTH CENTURY. FRESCO, CHURCH OF THE APHENTICO, MISTRA.

the high quality of the surviving fragments makes us regret all the more keenly the loss of so many noble works of art.

Enough, however, still exists for us to distinguish the work of several groups of craftsmen, each with methods and traditions of its own, operating simultaneously or successively, whether in separate churches or in separate parts of the same decorative scheme. Mistra differs from Serbia in possessing no thirteenth-century work displaying the boldly innovating tendencies we found at Sopocani; quite possibly the purely Greek atmosphere prevailing at Mistra rendered the artists, whether consciously or not, less amenable to the new art ventures then in progress in France and Italy than were their contemporaries working in the palaces of the Serbian kings near the Dalmatian coast. At Mistra this conservative approach to art persisted in the paintings made there in the fourteenth century, but we must not forget that this applies to all the works of art produced in Orthodox countries at the time. Amongst the best mural paintings at Mistra are the frescos in the Aphentico Church (also called the Hodigitria Brontocheion) and those in two other churches of the Virgin, the Peribleptos and the Pantanassa. The frescos in the first two churches are dated to the fourteenth century, the decorations in the Pantanassa were made a century later.

In a chapel annexed to the Aphentico Church is a delightful panel depicting a group of martyrs in prayer, with handsome patricians in garments of many skillfully blended colors in the front row. Despite its somewhat studied elegance, this composition (which is in the manner of Kahrieh Djami and the School of Constantinople) does not lack emotion; the look of ecstasy on the faces of the young Greek aristocrats is well conceived and rendered.

As usual, the apse of the choir is decorated with portraits of canonized bishops, liturgists and theologians. That of St Gregory, "the Illuminator of Armenia," here reproduced, while an excellent example of these finely decorative figures, has a particular charm, due to the pinkish glow bathing the bishop's sacerdotal robes.

At the Peribleptos one of the large pictures in the Gospel cycle is a *Nativity* which might well be an icon on wood transposed

ST GREGORY OF GREAT ARMENIA. FOURTEENTH CENTURY.
FRESCO, CHURCH OF THE APHENTICO, MISTRA.

on to a vault, such is the luster of the colors, the decorative richness of the pattern of pinkish yellow rocks, drooping like clusters of flowers, amongst which lies the Virgin clad in a dark garment, with the Child beside her. All around are small figures hastening forward, adoring, floating in the air. This is a delightful example of the last, essentially Greek manner in favor when Byzantium and the Empire were on the brink of catastrophe and art took refuge in a dream-world.

A close-up view of a detail in *The Raising of Lazarus* enables us to appreciate the better the fresco-painter's meticulous technique; indeed he seems to forget that he is dealing with an extended wall surface, and not with the illustration of a manuscript. In a monumental setting such delicate handling of colors and forms, the dainty arabesques of the garments and the make-believe agitation of all these tiny figures seem a little out of keeping. True, this is a charming picture, in the best tradition. But it also shows that shortly before the fall of Byzantium procedures appropriate to monumental painting were losing ground to those more suited to the icon.

THE RAISING OF LAZARUS. FIFTEENTH CENTURY. FRESCO, CHURCH OF THE PANTANASSA, MISTRA.

ST MATTHEW THE EVANGELIST, THE ANCIENT OF DAYS, TWO CHERUBIM, ABRAHAM
AND ISAAC. ELEVENTH CENTURY. MS GREC 74, BIBLIOTHÈQUE NATIONALE, PARIS.

PAINTING IN BOOKS

It was in the sixth century that pictures on sacred subjects began to figure frequently on portable objects, including books. Paintings in manuscripts had this in common with the images on vases, caskets and articles of furniture, that they too served as decorations of specific objects and, as such, were obliged to adjust their forms to these, the art of every miniature being necessarily functional to the book containing it (though the extent to which it was thus conditioned varied). In fact the basic difference between a miniature and other kinds of decoration is its subordination, real or ostensible, to a given text; since the very conception of a book implies predominance of the written word. Generally speaking, this holds good even when the illuminations of a manuscript take up more space than the text, and when they are more than mere iconographical reflections of its content. The predominance of the written matter over the picture is most marked when the illustrations are huddled into margins, or relegated to front pages, preceding the book proper. Even when a frame surrounding a picture gives it an air of greater independence, its place is still determined by the lay-out of the text. And the preponderance of the latter is even more apparent when a decorative function is assigned to individual letters which, while still forming words, take part in the decoration of the page and, as a result, approximate to real illustrations.

Every miniature, in short, is subordinated to the book it illustrates in two ways; firstly, its theme is almost always dictated by the text and, secondly, its form is determined by the lay-out of the written page. Each Byzantine illuminator took his own line in meeting these requirements, though naturally enough he was chary of departing from a long-established tradition as to the method of illustrating manuscripts and the general aspect of a book containing text and illustrations. And when the history of the Byzantine miniature comes to be written, it will have much to say about the interplay of these two factors.

Amongst the oldest Byzantine manuscripts there are three—the handsomest that have come down to us—in which the vellum is tinted purple. Thus all the paintings stand out on a ground of vibrant color (it varies slightly from one page to another), which, far from being neutral, strikes the dominant note in the color-scheme. Each detail tells out against this purplish-red backcloth, whose warmth is communicated to scenes and figures, and whose only parallel is to be found in the gold backgrounds of mosaics. And gold, like purple, obviously called for pure, resonant hues or, alternatively, cool, bright colors such as blues and bluish whites.

In one of these purple manuscripts, the Vienna *Genesis*, the pictures are displayed in the lower margins of pages, opposite the text. They are small paintings, with or without frames, in which figures or scenes of domestic life are placed in landscape settings or in some cases against skies flushed with the light of dawn. Several artists worked on this picture sequence which, closely following the Bible narrative, almost reminds us of a documentary film. There is a pleasing lightness of touch and delicacy in these paintings, which are still strongly imbued with the conventions of classical art. The other two manuscripts in this group, both Gospels, have much in common. But unlike the fragment of the Gospel according to St Matthew known as the Sinope fragment (at the Bibliothèque Nationale, Paris) in which the illustrations interlock with the text, as in the Vienna *Genesis*, all the illustrations in the Rossano Gospel Codex (Treasure of the Cathedral, Rossano, Calabria) are grouped on special pages preceding the written text. In both manuscripts figures of Old Testament prophets accompany the Gospel scenes, thus visually enforcing the lesson inscribed on scrolls held up by the prophets: that the New Testament is the fulfillment of the Old. Here the illustrations are not anecdotal, but demonstrations of religious verities, and the uniform sobriety of the style is in keeping with this more exalted function; instead of the unselfconscious figures in the Vienna *Genesis*, we here see persons conscious of their audience, playing their parts like actors in a Mystery Play. They are lined out along a narrow strip of ground; landscape is eliminated and accessories are reduced to a minimum. Depth, too, is ruled out in these scenes, the relative positions of figures being indicated only in cases where they are in actual contact with each other. The page of the Rossano Gospel which illustrates the parable of the Wise and the Foolish Virgins is one of the best preserved. The obvious anxiety of the Foolish Virgins in their bright garments contrasts with the staid demeanor of the Wise, aggrandized and ennobled by their rectitude. Behind them Christ is closing the Gate of Paradise, a garden bathed in limpid light, in which we glimpse the four streams of living water and the white radiance of the Blessed.

On another page of the same Gospel are, one above the other, scenes of the Judgment of Pilate and Judas returning the thirty pieces of silver to the priests before hanging himself on a twisted tree. True, these are direct illustrations of famous passages in the Gospels. Yet it cannot have been the Gospel text alone that inspired the artist's rendering of the trial scene, its realistic details, its pomp and circumstance, with the Judge—not Christ—holding the center of the composition, and it is obvious that here the artist has resorted to the procedures of imperial art. Nevertheless it is Christ, and not the Judge, who, though prisoner at the bar, is arrayed in gold and has a kingly mien. And his ultimate triumph is made manifest, indeed stressed, by the ignominious end of Judas, his betrayer.

The precise dates and provenance of the Rossano Gospel and the other manuscripts on purple vellum are unknown. While all alike are sixth-century works, it does not follow that they were made at the same date or in the same workshops. And although there are no *a priori* grounds for rejecting Constantinople as their place of origin, the color of the vellum—purple—does not necessitate their attribution to the imperial *scriptoria*. For it was the use of red ink for the signature, not the hue of the paper or vellum, that was the Emperor's prerogative. Evocative though they are of imperial pomp, there can be no doubt that the purple pages and gold- and silver-written texts of these Gospels are solely a homage to the Divine Ruler of the Universe and thus have no associations with the earthly seat of Empire.

Apart from the manuscripts on purple vellum, only one surviving sixth-century book has paintings of high artistic value in considerable numbers. This is the "Rabula Gospel," the text of which was written in 586 in a convent (Zagba) in Northern Mesopotamia, near the frontier of the Byzantine Empire. Though this Gospel is in the Syriac language, its illustrations are obviously in the Greek spirit, and this is why we include one of them. In this *Ascension* the form of Christ ascending recalls Ezekiel's vision of God the Father, and the emotion of the Virgin and apostles gazing awe-struck at the celestial miracle is well conveyed by their attitudes and gestures. At once dramatic and realistic in its treatment of details (e.g. faces and arms), this picture owes to the classical tradition, which had persisted well into the Christian Era, its use, limited though this is, of perspective both linear and aerial (i.e. gradations of tone due to the distance of objects) and of foreshortening; also its telling representation of a cloudy sky. Yet, despite affiliations with classical Antiquity, the Rabula Gospel points the way towards the mediaeval Byzantine miniature more directly than the Gospels on purple vellum—the main reason for this being that the characteristically Near-Eastern (Palestinian) iconography followed in the framed miniatures such as this *Ascension*, as also in the vignettes on the margins of the pages devoted to the Canons of Concordance, was destined to play a leading part in art forms of the Middle Ages.

No Byzantine book that can be positively ascribed to the period extending from the seventh to the mid-ninth century has survived. True, some have tentatively dated to the seventh century the charming illuminations in the *Book of Job* (in Patmos), and to the period of the Iconoclasts (727-843) several manuscripts in the Bibliothèque Nationale, Paris. But all these books (those in Paris especially) may well be subsequent to 843, as are the numerous illustrated manuscripts we shall now discuss.

It was (as stated in the Introduction) after the iconoclastic interregnum that the flowering of the art of the illuminated book took place; judging by its oldest examples, it did not make an effective start until the beginning of the ninth century, and by this time the new generation of painters was mainly occupied in laying the foundations of an art that had been banned for a century and more by the Iconoclasts.

A group of Psalters (of the type known as "Khludov Psalters," after a manuscript in the Moscow Public Library) may be taken as our first example of this initial stage in the evolution of the illuminated book after Iconoclasm. The margins are lined with hundreds of tiny pictures and, like glosses on a text, each has a mark referring the reader to the passage it interprets. Illustrations in the exact sense of the term, such tiny vignettes had been in use before the iconoclast period and were merely revived and improved on in the ninth century. This, indeed, is proved by their execution, which keeps to the methods and technique of the last phase of Antiquity. Some fragments of a fifth-century Alexandrian Chronicle on papyrus (Public Library, Moscow) have illustrations very similar both as regards the disposal of the pictures in relation to the text and even their style; these pictures have, in fact, retained something of what the oldest paintings of this type set out to be: hasty sketches jotted on the margin of the page to implement the message of the text.

THE JUDGMENT OF PILATE. SIXTH CENTURY. CODEX PURPUREUS.
CATHEDRAL TREASURE, ROSSANO.

PARABLE OF THE WISE AND FOOLISH VIRGINS. SIXTH CENTURY. CODEX PURPUREUS. CATHEDRAL TREASURE, ROSSANO.

Cosmas Indicopleustes, a sixth-century writer, made his own illustrations for his *Topographia Christiana*. But the earliest available copy of this book is dated as late as the ninth century (Vatican Library, MS Graec. 699). These paintings are quite unlike those in the margins of the Psalters, though they, too, reproduce pre-iconoclast originals. Also, they are placed within the written page, not on its margins, and, curiously enough perhaps, the effect of this lay-out is to widen the gap between text and picture, as compared with the system of marginal illustrations. For it is simpler to place a marginal picture alongside the passage it refers to than to intercalate a picture that necessarily breaks up the flow of the text. The reason is that a vignette thus inserted is bound to precede or succeed the text it illustrates, whereas in the case of marginal pictures text and illustration march side by side. In short the intercalation of vignettes in the text itself could but embarrass the reader—unless the lay-out made it clear that the pictures were to be viewed as independent units. This, in fact, was done by Cosmas; his portraits of biblical characters are isolated by blank spaces, while groups and scenes are framed in bands of color, marking off rectangles of the appropriate dimensions from the rest of the page.

As in the Psalters mentioned above, the treatment of the paintings in the *Topographia* conforms to the practice of the last centuries of Antiquity. Their kinship with

THE ASCENSION. RABULA GOSPEL. BIBLIOTECA LAURENZIANA, FLORENCE.

the pictures in the Psalters is apparent above all in the drawing and modeling of figures and drapery. But Cosmas retained more features of the classical prototypes than did the makers of the Psalters; notable being his reproductions of the architectural backgrounds of Hellenistic landscapes, with all the buildings in correct perspective, diminishing in size according to their distance from the spectator. But what gives these ninth-century replicas of pictures made three centuries earlier their historical value is the general aspect of these nobly hieratic compositions, their harmonious (if somewhat monotonous) rhythm. Here we have the same aesthetic as that of such indisputably sixth-century works as the Rossano Gospel and, notably, the mosaics of the Justinian era. Nevertheless the version of this style found in the Vatican Cosmas also adumbrates the most typical Byzantine paintings of the tenth and eleventh centuries, and thus the art of these miniatures furnishes one of the most striking proofs of the continuity of the Byzantine tradition from the close of Antiquity to the Middle Ages.

It is obvious that this painter paid no great heed to elegance, whether as regards the proportions of the human body, or gestures, or the attire of his figures. This holds good also for the faces, which lack not only charm but often spiritual nobility. This seems all the more surprising when we remember that the function of the robust, prosaic art of the ninth century was to voice the enthusiasm felt by the defenders of Christian imaging after their triumph in 843. But, as often happens in such cases, there was a time-lag; the doctrine of the sanctity of the image found an adequate expression

EZEKIEL'S VISION. CA. 880. SERMONS OF ST GREGORY OF NAZIANZUS, MS GREC 510,
BIBLIOTHÈQUE NATIONALE, PARIS.

ORTHODOX CHRISTIANS FLEEING FROM THE ARIANS. CA. 880. SERMONS OF ST GREGORY OF NAZIANZUS, MS GREC 510, BIBLIOTHÈQUE NATIONALE, PARIS.

in art only in the tenth and eleventh centuries. It was then, too, that the Byzantine love of glowing color came into its own—whereas the austere depiction of the Conversion of St Paul in the Vatican Cosmas brings to mind a tinted bas-relief. And, likewise as in a bas-relief, successive scenes of the same incident were shown simultaneously, leaving it to the spectator to arrange them in their chronological order. None the less the painter had done some preliminary spade-work so to speak for the spectator's benefit; the various episodes were grouped in such a way as to stress the most important incident, and at the same time form on organic whole. And the Byzantine mediaeval artists turned to wonderful account this technique of pivoting the lines of force upon a central axis and thus concentrating the impact of the composition.

It was in the 'eighties of the ninth century and at Constantinople that the famous copy of the sermons of St Gregory of Nazianzus, now in the Bibliothèque Nationale, Paris (MS Grec 510), was made for the Emperor Basil I, founder of the Macedonian dynasty. Over forty folio pictures, some in a rather damaged state, are intercalated between the manuscript pages. Much larger than the general run of Byzantine "miniatures," these paintings have always ranked as masterpieces of Byzantine art. Moreover they are of much importance historically, since they show what the most favorably placed artists at Constantinople, in a period that was to have a decisive influence on

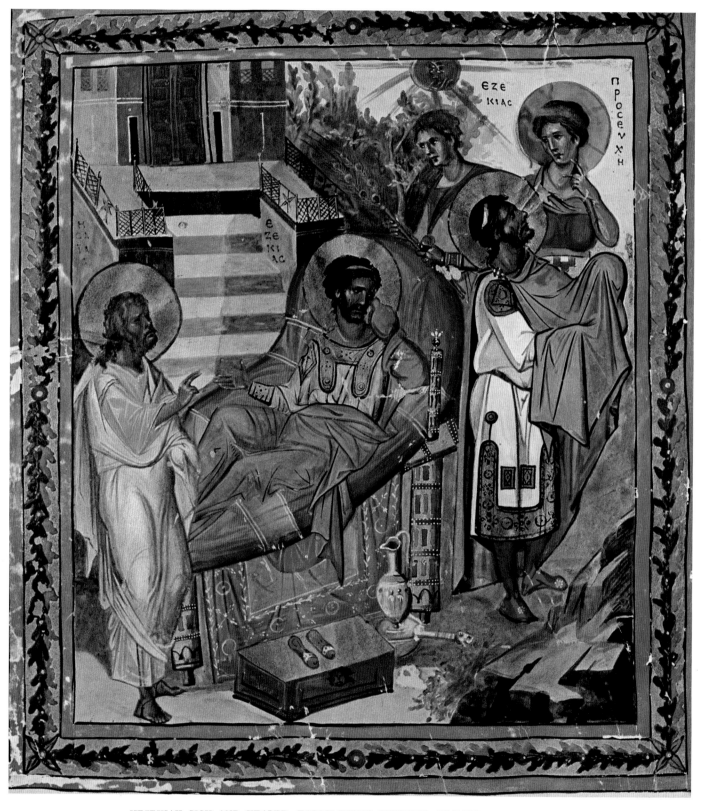

HEZEKIAH SICK AND HEALED. EARLY TENTH CENTURY. PSALTER, MS GREC 139,
BIBLIOTHÈQUE NATIONALE, PARIS.

THE CROSSING OF THE RED SEA. EARLY TENTH CENTURY. PSALTER, MS GREC 139,
BIBLIOTHÈQUE NATIONALE, PARIS.

the whole course of mediaeval art, found most rewarding—as regards technical procedures—in the available repertory of forms and iconographic patterns.

For even a cursory examination of the pictures makes it clear that round about 880—approximately half a century after the end of "official" Iconoclasm—the artists employed by the Emperor in the capital had not so far struck out a style of their own, and, like the illustrators of the Khludov Psalters and the Vatican Cosmas, still contented themselves with reproducing more or less faithfully the paintings in pre-iconoclastic manuscripts; in other words, that figural painting in books was still marking time in Byzantium throughout this period.

The paintings in Paris MS Grec 510 clearly show the influence of art trends of different origins and periods. Thus there are scenes recalling the curt anecdotal sketches in the Khludov Psalters (e.g. the story of Joseph) and alongside these are other scenes, likewise anecdotal, but much more detailed and carefully executed (illustrating the history of the Church in the fourth century); and, again, there are pictures which instead of telling a story invite us to contemplate, not only prophets, apostles and saints, but also manifestations of God Himself (Theophanies to the prophets; the Transfiguration, Pentecost). Without discussing here the sources of these paintings—which are not invariably

MOSES RECEIVING THE TABLES OF THE LAW. BIBLE OF LEO THE PATRICIAN, REG. SVEV. GRAEC. I, VATICAN LIBRARY, VATICAN CITY.

170

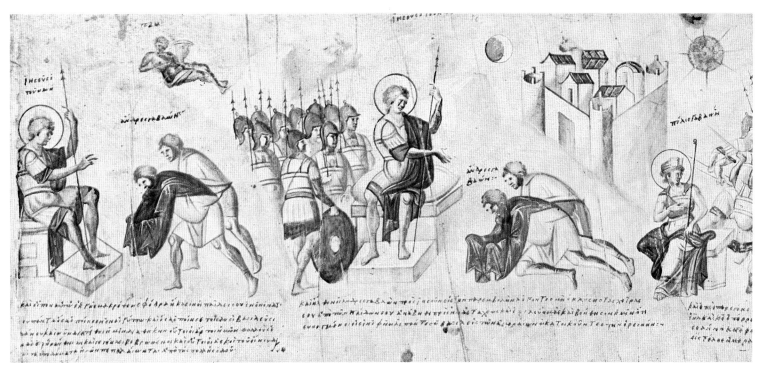

JOSHUA AND THE TWO SPIES. TENTH CENTURY. JOSHUA ROLL, MS PALAT. GRAEC. 431,
VATICAN LIBRARY, VATICAN CITY.

to be traced to earlier miniatures, since some of the pictures in MS Grec 510, notably
the large scenes of "visions," have more in common with murals of the same period—
we may draw attention to two vignettes which, exceptionally, seem to stem from the
tradition of the illustrated book, with which we are here concerned.

The first, taken from the series of biblical visions, is a detail of the picture of
Ezekiel in the Valley of Dry Bones. We see him led by an angel, gazing at the bones;
then in prayer, invoking the miracle which will transform the bones into living men.
Here the painter (circa 880) follows very closely a painting in a much earlier manuscript
(dated to before the sixth century), to which he owes that delicate blush-pink of the
sky at daybreak, the Alpenglow on the mountain-tops, and, even more, the "impressionist" execution of this work, in which contour-lines are almost wholly absent.
It is not (as usual in the Middle Ages) from a clearly demarcated sector of the sky but
from a patch of various shades of blue that God's hand descends upon the prophet.

Were there only the landscape, we might well have ascribed this picture to the
close of classical Antiquity. The figures, however, are patently the work of a ninth-
century artist, who achieves his excellent rendering of the draped figure only at the cost
of all-too-obvious efforts—whereas the faces already bear the stamp of a spirituality
that is typically mediaeval. No other indisputably Byzantine work comes so close
to the Castelseprio frescos.

The scenes in the same manuscript relating to the religious history of the Empire
in the fourth century are very different in spirit. Though we cannot feel certain that

(as some have alleged) they are copies of illustrations in the *Historia Ecclesiastica* (by Sozomen, Socrates or Theodoret), there is no question that their prototypes were ancient. Thus the original of the deeply moving scene we reproduce was most likely a fifth-century depiction of a tragic incident in the persecution of the Orthodox Christians by the Arians (an incident not mentioned by the historians named above). A bishop, a priest, a monk and some laymen are gazing at the rising flames, lit by the Arians, that will soon consume the little boat (on which they have probably been forcibly embarked) and its human freight. The realistic attitudes, gestures and faces, even the squat figures are much more reminiscent of the pictures in the Khludov Psalters and the Vatican Cosmas than of the art of *Ezekiel's Vision*, which, however, figures in the same book. Yet this was the art that was to prevail, in the immediate future, in the Byzantine illuminated manuscript—which, from the early tenth century on, was destined to be the principal beneficiary of the revival of classical taste.

No more brilliant illustration exists of this classicizing tendency in the art of the Byzantine miniature than the Psalter in the Bibliothèque Nationale, Paris (MS Grec 139), assuredly the most famous of all Greek illustrated manuscripts. With it may be associated two other manuscripts with classical illustrations: first, the Bible of Leo the Patrician at the Vatican (Reg. Svev. Graec. 1) which reproduces several paintings of the Psalter, and second, very different though it is, the celebrated "Joshua Roll" in the same library (MS Palat. Graec. 431). The Paris Psalter is illustrated with full-page paintings in lavishly decorated frames. The subjects and iconographical arrangement of these pictures go as far back as the *Ezekiel's Vision* (Paris MS Grec 510), that is to say to the first centuries of the Christian Empire. Moreover the "Ezekiel" here has much affinity with the "Isaiah" in the Psalter (scene with Ezekiel); thus Paris MS Grec 139 cannot be greatly later than Paris MS Grec 510, the differences between the two being due less to their respective dates than to the models followed by their respective illustrators. The imitations of ancient prototypes made by the artists responsible for Paris MS Grec 139 (there were several, and of greatly varying caliber) are the best we know of (for the Middle Ages)—which goes to prove a familiarity with classical works that could have been acquired, so far as can be judged, only in certain *milieux* of the capital. True, these imitations of classical art are labored; but the best, two of which we reproduce, are more than literal copies; the scenes are re-arranged in centripetal compositions, as in the Cosmas manuscript and the series of "visions" in Paris MS Grec 510. Also, the pensive, sometimes "melting" gaze of the protagonists in the Bible story, as well as the brightness and variety of colors belong both to the Byzantine painting of the period and, in part, to that of the illustrations in Paris MS Grec 139. Both the pictures we reproduce—*Hezekiah Sick and Healed* and *The Crossing of the Red Sea*—bring out the two directives of this art: fidelity to classical models and a striving for sumptuous effect.

In the Vatican Bible we often find interpretations of the same models as those of the Paris Psalter, and sometimes more spontaneous reproductions of their forms. In the scene of *Moses receiving the Tables of the Law*, the rocky landscape, the toponymical personification in the foreground and the group of Israelites have the liveliness of an ancient work. Yet, unlike the best painters in Paris MS Grec 139, this artist, capable though he was of making so skillful a copy of an ancient painting, was unable to avoid grotesque distortions when representing hurried movement, and faulty proportions in foreshortenings of limbs.

An indirect commemoration, maybe, of the triumphs of Byzantine arms in Palestine during the tenth century, the Joshua Roll depicts in unbroken sequence the exploits of Joshua as narrated in Holy Writ, with the appropriate texts written in at the foot of the pictures. This artist was no less faithful to classical tradition than were the painters of the two books discussed above; indeed he shows an even greater feeling for the delicate grace of classical line. Also, by keeping to the early manner of the colored sketch, he diverges radically from those contemporaries of his whose chief concern was brilliant color effects. For the rest, however, following in the footsteps of the painters of the Psalters and Bibles, he endeavors to impart an ordered rhythm to the "frieze" of antique pictures reproduced. We can gauge his success by the symmetry and just proportions here achieved, which,

THERIACA OF NICANDER. TENTH CENTURY.
MS GREC 247, BIBLIOTHÈQUE NATIONALE, PARIS.

THE ARCHANGEL MICHAEL. CA. 1000. MENOLOGION OF BASIL II, MS GRAEC. 1613, VATICAN LIBRARY.

without conflicting with classical aesthetic tradition, conform to the Byzantine. Indeed what we have here is no more than retouchings of an ancient prototype. Just as Byzantine scholars of the period brought out versions of classical texts that were superior to those of Late Antiquity, so the painter of the Joshua Roll and some of the painters responsible for Paris MS Grec 139 were more successful in giving their work an authentically classical aspect than were their *confrères*, the painters in the large and sculptors of the Early Byzantine Epoch and the first post-iconoclast decades.

Given the prevailing interest in classical art it was natural that non-religious books, as well, should be adorned with pictures. Actually, however, only a few such manuscripts seem to have been made, though the paintings in them—a notable example being Nicander's *Theriaca*, a treatise on snake-bites (Bibliothèque Nationale, Paris, MS Grec 247)—are of great beauty. In any case the Byzantines made few original contributions to these books; in the Nicander manuscript the artist merely copied the originals and even kept to a brown-and-blue color-scheme and an angular linework not found elsewhere in authentically Byzantine works.

PICTURES OF SAINTS. EARLY ELEVENTH CENTURY. MS GREC 64,
BIBLIOTHÈQUE NATIONALE, PARIS.

In some manuscripts of the second half of the tenth century (Paris MS Grec 70) or of the early eleventh (Paris MS Grec 64) we trace the beginnings of a style, peculiar to this period, which was to flourish in the eleventh and even as late as the twelfth century. This style reveals not only an assimilation of the lessons of ancient painting but also the adaptation of its means of expression to the spirit and the religious themes in favor at Byzantium. The first of these manuscripts, a Gospel, is a charming little work made to the order of some connoisseur. In his picture of St Matthew, the painter stresses plastic values and the third dimension; in fact the figure of the evangelist on its gold background brings to mind an image in relief on a book-cover.

In the portraits of saints in Paris MS Grec 64 the tendencies we perceive in Paris MS Grec 70 are carried a stage farther. Figures are elongated, garments more schematic and more closely wedded to bodies; the faces, too, have intimations of that ascetic ideal which was to prevail in the eleventh century. In this book we also find not only brilliant colors (as in Paris MS Grec 139) but decorative patterns covering whole pages and combining sacred images, and sometimes pagan ornamental motifs with a calligraphic text. This second combination becomes more generalized from now on, being used for frontispieces and more particularly on

DECORATIVE COMPOSITION. EARLY ELEVENTH CENTURY. CANON OF CONCORDANCE, MS GREC 64, BIBLIOTHÈQUE NATIONALE, PARIS.

pages devoted to the "Canons of Concordance" of the Gospels. Thus in the margins we find again those scenes of games and hunting, the plants, animals and monsters which at the beginning of the Byzantine era figured in floor mosaics in palaces and villas, and also on articles of furniture. The architectural decorations of the Canons stemmed from the decorative architecture of the Islamic lands and imitated the delicately wrought enamel-work which had been in favor at Constantinople from the ninth century on. These bold chromatic juxtapositions and combinations of patches of almost strident color with gold grounds were certainly inspired by the art of the enamelers. Owing much to the East, this technique brought with it many Iranian motifs; thus the influence of enamel-work on painting also involved the influence of eastern arts. Other applied arts, such as the patterned textiles of Persia and other Mohammedan lands, and their Byzantine imitations, had the same effect and supplied the book illustrators with oriental flower and animal patterns. But it was chiefly the headpieces, vignettes and historiated initial letters that benefited by these contacts. Thus the practice of lavish ornamentation in illuminated manuscripts established itself in Byzantium somewhat later than in the Latin countries, under the Macedonian dynasty, and probably under the influence of oriental art techniques. And a curious feature of the Byzantine illuminated book at the close of the ninth century and in the tenth is that we so often find strongly classicizing paintings combined with elaborate decorative motifs of unequivocally Eastern inspiration.

The series of eleventh-century illustrated books begins with the famous Menologion (Vatican MS Graec. 1613) of the Emperor Basil II (976-1025). To each day of the liturgical calendar is assigned an image, a saint's portrait, a scene of martyrdom and sometimes the Gospel incident commemorated by the Church festival allotted to the day. In these small pictures, which—this is an exception at Byzantium—are signed (by five Court painters), we have the culmination of

WORK IN THE FIELDS. ELEVENTH CENTURY. MS GREC 74, BIBLIOTHÈQUE NATIONALE, PARIS.

that effort to harmonize the lessons of the past with contemporary taste, whose earliest achievements can be seen in Paris MS Grec 64. In the Menologion this synthesis is perfect in its kind, and indicates at once the virtues and the limitations of the aesthetic program of the paintings of this period. Admirable in any case is the unity of expression we find: figures, surrounding objects, landscapes of hills and buildings— everything within the picture space implements this unity; thus the hills reiterate the gesture of the leading figure, while the line of his uplifted arm is repeated in the outline of a nearby building. The Byzantine handling of these procedures tends less towards the arabesque than to a sort of anthropomorphism, in which pride of place is invariably given to the human figure and, in the man himself, to all that signifies his inner life.

In the tenth century (as already noted) the small de-luxe book, catering to the taste of the rich connoisseur and a favored few, made its first appearance. Distinguished chiefly by the small size of the paintings and their delicate execution (i.e. by the technical skill of the craftsmen concerned), these were produced in greater numbers during the eleventh and twelfth centuries. It is in these small books for connoisseurs, all of them made in Constantinople itself, that we have the earliest known examples of Gospels so copiously illustrated that there is a picture on practically every page. Paris MS Grec 115 is the oldest, Paris MS Grec 74 the handsomest and best preserved. What first strikes us is the intricate decoration of the frontispieces, in which tiny figures are intermingled with ornamental details imitating enamel-work. But yet more noteworthy is the great number of illustrations and the part they play in the over-all decorative effect of each page. Evidently these tiny vignettes were made by highly expert artists; we need but observe how skillfully one of them has exploited the decorative possibilities of the growing vine and another those of a group of birds and plants. Sometimes, no doubt, the pictures *qua* works of art may seem monotonous and inexpressive—mere stop-gaps to keep the flow of images continuous; nevertheless, their decorative effect, vivid colors and embellishments in gold amply compensate for these shortcomings. In some cases, however, the artists have succeeded in imparting to forms and gestures, and even to facial expressions (notably in scenes of the Passion), intimations of human dignity or suffering that exalt these diminutive images above the genre to which, in other respects, they naturally belong.

While some monastic group of craftsmen was at work on the decorations of Paris MS Grec 74, another group, perhaps in the Imperial Palace, was making the few paintings in Coislin 79 (Bibliothèque Nationale, Paris), all of which figure on the frontispiece of a volume of sermons by St John Chrysostom, and show the Emperor Nicephorus Botaniates (1078-1081) accepting this book. Thus we can fix the exact date, within a year or so, of these paintings and, both historically and aesthetically, they constitute a landmark in the annals of the illustrated manuscript. Pertinent in regard to them are the observations made above as to the influence of enamel-work and figured textiles on the miniatures of this period, the "orientalism" which, by way of these techniques, had crept into Byzantine painting, and, *per contra*, the ascetic ideals which steadily

ST JOHN CHRYSOSTOM PRESENTING THE EMPEROR NICEPHORUS BOTANIATES WITH HIS COLLECTED SERMONS. BETWEEN 1078 AND 1081. SERMONS OF ST JOHN CHRYSOSTOM. COISLIN 79, BIBLIOTHÈQUE NATIONALE, PARIS.

gained ground from the eleventh century on. All these tendencies are visible in the picture here reproduced, which clearly illustrates the penchant of the Imperial Court during this period for lavish ornamentation, exotic techniques, and the oriental motifs they brought in with them.

Anonymous like all the rest, but possessing an outstanding personality, a twelfth-century Byzantine painter invented a whole set of new pictures for a collection of sermons on the Virgin by the monk Jacobus of Kokkinobaphos. Two copies of this book, with the same illustrations, exist : in the Bibliothèque Nationale, Paris, and in the Vatican. The four miniatures we reproduce are in the former (MS Grec 1208). Most of these paintings are in a remarkably fine state of preservation; indeed the view of *Paradise and the Four Rivers* and the *Ark of the Covenant above the Suitors of Mary* have a brightness of color (evident in our reproductions) which might suggest that these twelfth-century paintings were at some time "restored." I can assure my readers of the contrary; they have undergone no alteration whatsoever.

New illustrations were rarely made at Byzantium in the Middle Ages, and the creations of the painter with whom we are now concerned must be regarded as an exception to the rule. However, their novelty was only partial, since many familiar Gospel scenes, such as Pentecost, the Ascension, apocryphal episodes in the Life of the Virgin, figure amongst them. Nor did the artist hesitate about enriching his work with pictures and ornamental motifs (e.g. the frontispiece in the form of a church) culled from other illustrated books. Sometimes, nevertheless, he departed from these prototypes and gave free rein to his creative fancy. There is a very real splendor in his visions of these fantastic scenes; his Paradise is a world of shimmering gold, guarded by cherubim, full of strange trees and leafage and irrigated by four jets of water

issuing from a red tube shouldered by a celestial gardener. On the other hand, according to this painter, it is enough for two angels to uplift the vast and spangled curtain of the sky for the Ancient of Days and the myriads of the angelic hosts to be revealed. We can also discern the very real originality of this artist in the exceptional boldness of the colors; for though bright tones are often used in mediaeval Byzantine illustrated books, they rarely attain such intensity, nor do we find such daring clashes of blues and reds, of reds and browns. Likewise, the striped *papilio* (tent) is a *tour de force* outside the run of ordinary Byzantine practice. As a matter of fact several twelfth-century Byzantine painters seem to have had a taste for innovations. In the manuscript with which we are concerned these are of a purely plastic and iconographic order; in the contemporary Nerezi frescos, on the other hand, the novelty was the artist's practice of a powerfully emotive realism. In fact the artistic climate of this century (in Byzantium) favored originality in all fields of art, frescos, mosaics and the illuminated book.

Like all the costlier arts, that of the de-luxe illustrated book suffered by the economic and political decline of the Greek Empire after the sack of Constantinople by the Crusaders in 1204; thus Byzantine miniatures of the thirteenth and fourteenth centuries seldom attain the level of the older works. There are, however, some noteworthy exceptions; amongst them the full-page paintings in a collection of the theological treatises of the Emperor John VI Cantacuzenos (1347-1354). Here, alongside a *Transfiguration*, we are given a double portrait, somewhat in the manner of an icon, of the imperial author, first in kingly apparel, then in the garb of a monk (he had

been driven out of Constantinople and had retired to a monastery where he was devoting himself to literary labors at the time when this manuscript was made). The skillfully contrived execution of these portraits, sadly damaged though they are, compels our admiration and proves that book-illustration was still a living art in Byzantium. It also shows that this artist—quite possibly of set purpose—broke with the antique tradition; hence the total lack of expressiveness, the absence of effective plastic values, in the body beneath its garments, in striking contrast with the remarkable vitality of the head in each portrait. But it must be admitted that neither this painting—nor indeed any other in books produced in the period of the Palaeologi—has any outstanding aesthetic merit.

During this period only mural painting (in churches) still continued to make headway and alongside it, in the field of panel-painting, it was no longer the

THE ARK OF THE COVENANT ABOVE THE SUITORS OF MARY. TWELFTH CENTURY. SERMONS ON THE VIRGIN BY JACOBUS OF KOKKINOBAPHOS, MS GREC 1208, BIBLIOTHÈQUE NATIONALE, PARIS.

GOD AND THE ANGELIC HOST. TWELFTH CENTURY.
SERMONS ON THE VIRGIN BY
JACOBUS OF KOKKINOBAPHOS, MS GREC 1208,
BIBLIOTHÈQUE NATIONALE, PARIS.

miniature that flourished, but the icon, painted or in mosaic.

In this connection it is interesting to observe the fundamental change that had now taken place in the relations between illuminations in books and wall painting in the large, not only frescos but mosaics. Under the rule of the Macedonians and the Comneni, miniatures had had the monumental air of images suitable for decorating the walls of buildings; even the smallest illustration in a manuscript of this period might be a small-scale reproduction of some mural painting. Under the Palaeologi the situation was reversed; in the thirteenth century and above all in the fourteenth and fifteenth centuries, most of the frescos figuring in churches and even some of the mosaics (those at Kahrieh Djami for example) give, rather, the impression of vastly enlarged manuscript illuminations. For we find in them the insistence on anecdotal elements and the scrupulous attention to detail which were normal and appropriate in the illustrations of texts; also the meticulous execution and finish typical of the Byzantine miniature throughout its long career.

In this respect the mural painters of the close of the Byzantine era went much farther than the makers of the mosaics in Santa Maria Maggiore in Rome and than those other Early Christian church decorators who adorned the walls of the basilicas with biblical scenes whose descriptive methods affiliated them more or less closely to miniatures. Indeed, when in the fourteenth century this tendency reappeared, it was carried to quite extraordinary lengths; at the expense (not invariably but all too frequently) of the over-all effect of the mural decorations in churches, though to the undoubted advantage of the didactic purpose these were intended to fulfill.

In fact, when we look at fourteenth-century frescos and mosaics—which often constitute entire picture-cycles, each consisting of a continuous sequence of images treated in a narrative spirit, that is to say with a view to furnishing the spectator with the fullest possible information about a biblical or hagiographical incident or personage—we can almost imagine we are gazing at the open pages of an enormous, lavishly illustrated book.

183

DOUBLE PORTRAIT OF THE EMPEROR JOHN VI CANTACUZENOS. BETWEEN 1347 AND 1354. HOMILIES OF THE
EMPEROR JOHN VI CANTACUZENOS, MS GREC 1242, BIBLIOTHÈQUE NATIONALE, PARIS.

Another interesting point is that the "legends" written on these pictures are for the most part passages, sometimes of considerable length, culled from Holy Writ or the liturgies; and there can be little doubt it was in illustrated versions of these, for the most part, that fourteenth-century painters found the models which they employed when composing their frescos and mosaics.

In other words, though during the last phase of Byzantine art portable paintings almost invariably took the form of the icon, and no longer that of the miniature, many of the most characteristic qualities of the miniature were given a new lease of life in the mural decorations of the period.

THE ARCHANGEL MICHAEL. TENTH CENTURY. ENAMEL ICON FROM A CHURCH IN CONSTANTINOPLE.
TREASURE OF ST MARK'S, VENICE.

ICONS

Originally, the Byzantines applied the name of "icon" to every depiction of Christ, the Virgin, a saint or an incident in Holy Writ, whether carved or painted, movable or monumental, and whatever the technique in which it was executed. The modern Orthodox Church, however, tends to restrict the use of the term to small movable pictures (other than those in illuminated manuscripts), and this is the meaning it always bears in archaeology and art history.

Thus the Byzantine icon may be defined as a representation of a sacred subject on a portable plaque of wood, stone or metal, no matter what the technique employed —painting on wood surfaced with plaster, enamel-work, or mosaic.

As mentioned in our Introduction, few icons painted with the brush on wood and belonging to the period properly termed Byzantine have survived, because, for one thing, such works were highly perishable. Another reason is that icons of this kind were not produced on a really large scale until the last centuries of the Eastern Empire and the period of Turkish domination. Thus few icons of the earliest period have come down to us, and even these are often inaccessible. They are mostly fifth- and sixth-century works emanating from Egyptian or Palestinian workshops and are done in tempera or in the encaustic technique; indeed they belong to an art that was "Byzantine" only in the broadest application of the term. Thus we omit them from the present work, and confine ourselves to icons that are Byzantine in the exact sense of the word and, owing to the fact of being made in materials less perishable than wood, or being later in date, have escaped the ravages of time. We would also refer the reader to our illustrations of certain mosaics and frescos which almost certainly were "enlargements" of famous icons. In particular I have in mind the portraits of St Demetrios in the church of that saint at Salonica, and that of St Abbacyr in Santa Maria Antiqua, Rome.

Enamels. The earliest enamel icons illustrated here are of the cloisonné type and date to the eleventh and twelfth centuries. Ordinarily enamels are classed with goldsmiths' work and the applied arts, as distinct from painting, but this distinction does not hold good for Byzantine art. In a sense the mosaics and the paintings in books might all be assimilated, no less than the enamels, to industrial, essentially decorative products; moreover, the religious function of all Byzantine panel-painting was identical, and a good many icons in enamel must have figured in Byzantine churches.

One of our illustrations shows a famous enamel of this kind, which once figured in a large, eleventh-century church at Constantinople. It has the dimensions and all the normal characteristics of a painted icon or an icon in relief, and depicts the archangel Michael. This is one of those typically Byzantine works which combine different materials and various techniques with a view to over-all effect. Here, however, the combination is somewhat original. The archangel's head and wings are in repoussé gold, his dalmatic in enamel and gold filigree, and his sleeves and wings are dappled with enamels which here, exceptionally, are applied to concave surfaces, on which their glowing,

RELIQUARY CROSS, OBVERSE. TWELFTH CENTURY. ENAMEL,
CATHEDRAL OF COSENZA.

RELIQUARY CROSS, REVERSE. TWELFTH CENTURY. ENAMEL,
CATHEDRAL OF COSENZA.

semi-transparent colors alternate with gold filaments depicting folds and plumage. Finally, placed around Michael are other ornaments in filigree and other pieces of enamel which play their part in an harmonious rhythmic orchestration.

The reliquary-cross in the Cathedral at Cosenza was made in the twelfth century. It is decorated on both sides with remarkably fine pictures done in enamel; small as they are and carefully adapted to the structure of a portable cross, each is a self-sufficient work of art, and differs only in respect of its dimensions from a picture of the same subject executed in fresco or mosaic. The uniformity of style pervading all Byzantine art is evidenced by the enamels, whose gold ground so closely resembles that of their monumental counterparts, the mosaics. Thus here the Christ Crucified on the obverse of the cross, where there is a uniform gold ground, reminds us of the mosaics illustrating the same theme at Chios and Daphni. Similarly the five scenes on the reverse—Christ Enthroned and the Evangelists—parallel the mosaics in the domes. Above all one is reminded of such richly colorful mosaics as those in Chios and Daphni, which indeed may owe the brilliance of their color to the influence of enamels. Seemingly it was in the eleventh century that the art of the Byzantine enamel reached its apogee and, as in other periods and other lands, the perfecting of a new technique and its success gave rise to new aesthetic ventures in other fields, amongst these being new departures in the methods of illuminating manuscripts during the eleventh and twelfth centuries and modifications in the color-schemes of some mosaics belonging to the same period.

Throughout the twelfth and thirteenth centuries Byzantine enamels enjoyed a popularity as well-deserved as it was widespread: from Georgia in Transcaucasia and Kiev to Italy and the Rhineland. Many enamels found their way from the capital to these regions, while some were made on the spot (in Georgia, in Russia and at Venice) after Constantinopolitan models.

Portable Mosaics. At the close of the Middle Ages, when the Byzantines had fallen on evil times and could but rarely allow themselves the luxury of large-scale mosaic murals, the same technique was used for icons on wood, tiny cubes of gold, silver and various colors being affixed to a panel coated with wax. Costly as were such icons, they were still within the means of a number of people, and these portable mosaics were usually made for private use. Doubtless their owners were persons of culture who could appreciate no less their artistic merits than the craftsmen's technical proficiency.

Probably there had always been portable mosaics—some tenth- and eleventh-century examples have survived—but their great vogue began only in the fourteenth. To the same period belongs the diptych now in the Opera del Duomo at Florence: a portable altar adorned with scenes of the twelve chief Feasts of the liturgical calendar. It is quite certain that this meticulously, almost laboriously executed mosaic was directly inspired by some similar painted icon. But since no painted icon of this kind and period (that of the Palaeologi) has survived, we have to fall back on contemporary frescos and

SIX OF THE GREAT FEASTS OF THE YEAR. FOURTEENTH CENTURY. PORTABLE MOSAIC,
OPERA DEL DUOMO, FLORENCE.   →

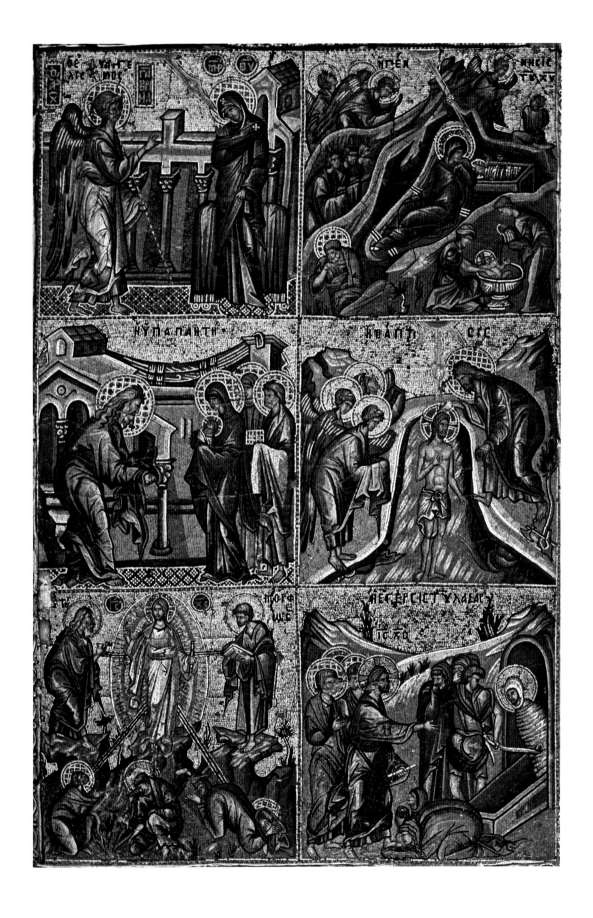

monumental mosaics (those in Kahrieh Djami, Gracanica or the Peribleptos at Mistra, for example) in order to "place" the style of the Florence icon. It is then seen to reflect the academic type of painting that flourished in Constantinople during the fourteenth century, of which it offers a dry, rather uninspired version. None the less the two-leaved icon at Florence is the finest example extant of the Byzantine portable mosaic.

Painting on Wood. We have already explained why perforce this kind of painting hardly figures at all in the present work. If our choice has fallen on a charming little painted icon (in the Benaki Museum, Athens), this is not because it is the most typical example of the genre, but merely because of its elegance and the charm of its colors. It bears no date, but may probably be assigned to the fourteenth century. The subject of this painting, the so-called "Old Testament Trinity," is the same as that of the detail on page 58; a comparison of the painting with the sixth-century mosaic throws light on the changes that had come over Byzantine art in the long interval. Stylistically it is akin to the frescos in the Peribleptos and the Pantanassa at Mistra (see pages 153-157), which as a matter of fact were obviously inspired by the aesthetic and technique of the portable icon.

ABRAHAM ENTERTAINING THE ANGELS. FOURTEENTH CENTURY (?) ICON, BENAKI MUSEUM, ATHENS.

BIBLIOGRAPHY
INDEX OF NAMES AND SUBJECTS
LIST OF COLORPLATES

BIBLIOGRAPHY

GENERAL

DIEHL, C. *Manuel d'Art byzantin*, Paris 1910; 2nd edition, Vols. I and II, 1925-1926.

DALTON, O. M. *Byzantine Art and Archaeology*, Oxford 1911.

WULFF, O. *Altchristliche und byzantinische Kunst*, Berlin 1914.

MILLET, G. *Recherches sur l'iconographie de l'Evangile*, Paris 1916.

STRZYGOWSKI, J. *Die bildende Kunst des Ostens*, Leipzig 1918.

DALTON, O. M. *East Christian Art*, Oxford 1925.

MURATOV, P. *La Peinture byzantine*, Paris 1928.

MOREY, C. R. *Early Christian Art*, Princeton 1942.

LASAREV, V. *History of Byzantine Painting* (in Russian), Vols. I and II, Moscow 1948.

WEITZMANN, K. *Greek Mythology in Byzantine Art*, Princeton 1951.

MOSAICS

MILLET, G. *Le Monastère de Daphni*, Paris 1899.

SCHMIT, T. *Kahrieh Djami* (in Russian), in Vols. VIII and IX, 1902 and 1906, of the *Izvestija* of the Russian Institute of Archaeology in Constantinople.

WILPERT, J. *Römische Mosaiken und Malereien*, Vols. I to IV, Freiburg-im-Breisgau 1916.

DIEHL, C.; LE TOURNEAU, F.; SALADIN. *Les Monuments chrétiens de Salonique*, Paris 1918.

DIEZ, E. and DEMUS, O. *Byzantine Mosaics in Greece*, Cambridge, Mass. 1931.

WHITTEMORE, T. *The Mosaics of St. Sophia at Istanbul*, Vols. I to IV, London 1933-1952.

BETTINI, S. *Mosaici antichi di San Marco a Venezia*, Bergamo 1944.

DEMUS, O. *The Mosaics of Norman Sicily*, London 1950.

XYNGOPOULOS, A. *Le décor en mosaïque de l'église des Saints-Apôtres à Thessalonique*, Salonica 1953.

FRESCOS

MILLET, G. *Monuments byzantins de Mistra*, Paris 1910.

GRÜNEISEN, W. de. *Sainte-Marie-Antique*, Rome 1911.

WILPERT, J. *Römische Mosaiken und Malereien*, Vols. I to IV, Freiburg-im-Breisgau 1916.

JERPHANION, G. de. *Les Eglises rupestres de Cappadoce* (4 vols. of text and 3 albums of plates), Paris 1925-1942.

OKUNEU, N. *Monumenta Artis Servicae*. Vols. I to IV. Prague, 1928-1932.

PETROVIC, V. *La Peinture serbe du Moyen Age*, Vols. I and II, Belgrade 1930, 1934.

The Excavations at Dura Europos. Preliminary Report of the Fifth Season; Sixth Season; Seventh and Eighth Seasons. New Haven 1934-1939.

MESNIL DU BUISSON, Comte du. *Les Peintures de la Synagogue de Doura Europos*, Rome 1939.

CHATZIDAKIS, M. *Mystras* (in Greek), Athens 1948.

BOGNETTI, G. P.; CHIERICI, G.; CAPITANI D'ARZAGO, A. de. *Santa Maria di Castelseprio*, Milan 1948.

MINIATURES

KONDAKOV, N. *Histoire de l'Art byzantin considéré principalement dans les Miniatures*, Vols. I and II, Paris 1886, 1891.

WICKHOFF, F. *Römische Kunst. Die Wiener Genesis*, Vienna 1895.

EBERSOLT, J. *La Miniature byzantine*, Paris 1926.

MOREY, C. R. *Notes on East Christian Miniatures*, in *The Art Bulletin*, XI, I, 1929.

WEITZMANN, K. *Die byzantinische Buchmalerei des IX. und X. Jahrhunderts*, Berlin 1935.

WEITZMANN, K. *Illustrations in Roll and Codex*, Princeton 1947.

WEITZMANN, K. *The Joshua Roll*, Princeton 1948.

ENAMELS

PASINI. *Il Tesoro di San Marco in Venezia*, Venice 1885.

KONDAKOV, N. *Emaux byzantins. Collection Zwenigorodskoï. Histoire et Monuments des Emaux byzantins*, Frankfurt-am-Main 1892.

ROSENBERG, M. *Geschichte der Goldschmiedekunst* (fascicles I to 6), Frankfurt-am-Main 1910-1925.

EBERSOLT, J. *Les Arts somptuaires de Byzance*, Paris 1923.

RIEGL, A. *Die spätrömische Kunstindustrie*, Vienna 1927.

ALFÖLDI, A. *Die Goldkanne von Saint-Maurice d'Agaune*, in *Zeitschrift für Schweizerische Archäologie und Kunstgeschichte*, 10, 1-2, 1948.

It may interest our readers to know that the Federal Institute for the Preservation of Ancient Monuments, Belgrade, will shortly issue a detailed monograph on the Church of St Sophia, Ochrid.

INDEX OF NAMES AND SUBJECTS

THE COLORPLATES